Preparing for Partnership:
A Guide to Achieving Partnership in a Law Firm

EDITED BY ALEX DAVIES

Commissioning editor
Alex Davies

Managing director
Sian O'Neill

Preparing for Partnership: A Guide to Achieving Partnership in a Law Firm
is published by

Globe Law and Business Ltd
3 Mylor Close
Horsell
Woking
Surrey GU21 4DD
United Kingdom
Tel: +44 20 3745 4770
www.globelawandbusiness.com

Preparing for Partnership: A Guide to Achieving Partnership in a Law Firm

ISBN: 978-1-78742-985-7
EPUB ISBN: 978-1-78742-986-4
Adobe PDF ISBN: 978-1-78742-987-1

Contents

Executive summary

Becoming a partner in a law firm is a significant milestone in a lawyer's career, and requires a combination of strong legal skills, business acumen, leadership abilities and a commitment to the firm's success.

The expectations of law firm partners are changing. Firms are increasingly looking for lawyers who can bring in new business, develop client relationships, and work collaboratively with others in the firm. Lawyers who have primarily focused on legal work in the past may need to develop new skills and competencies to meet these changing expectations.

This book outlines the critical factors for success, from building a strong track record to developing a loyal client base, demonstrating leadership skills and meeting the firm's criteria. Contributors to the book discuss how to network and build relationships within the firm, review the financial aspects of partnership, and how to seek feedback and mentorship from other partners.

In our opening chapter, Michael Roster outlines the issues that potential partners need to be aware of, from financial issues to work-life balance, to business development and beyond.

In chapter two, David Parnell looks at which types of firm offer the best chance of making partner. Imagine a spectrum; at one end is a practice that hasn't made a partner in over 20 years (Firm A); at the other is a practice that has made a partner in each of the last 20 years (Firm B). If you are an associate who's looking to make partner, would you rather be at Firm A or Firm B? This is, of course, a rhetorical question, but the scenario illustrates an important point – some firms are better predisposed to making partners. Or, otherwise said, some firms exhibit characteristics and attributes that can not only facilitate their making of partners, but are also earmarks or signals for the group's fertility. In this chapter, David considers some of these attributes and earmarks so that you, the hopeful associate, can make a better informed decision about the potential in your current group.

Demonstrating readiness and relevance for partnership is a key requirement for successful partnership; it's not just simply demonstrating a great "runup" year to partner in terms of productivity. Rather, a successful partner candidate must be able to show long-term commitment to the firm as well as a practice that aligns with the firm's strategy and client base. In chapter three, Jennifer Bluestein, chief talent and HR officer at Perkins Coie, looks at how to demonstrate readiness for partnership with a focus on client relationships and client development.

Often, whether or not associates progress to partnership comes down to choice. There is a choice to be made by the firm doing the promoting, but there is also a choice to be made by the individual themselves. The question, "Do I want to make partner?" is often something that professions struggle with. In chapter four, Claire Rason, director of Client Talk Ltd, explores some of the reasons why women in particular might choose not to progress. She examines the impact that this has on gender parity at partnership level and suggests how it can be addressed. What is behind these individual choices and how can we reframe the question?

A partner in a law firm has an extraordinarily complex and demanding role. A partner is expected to be the embodiment of an entire commercial business, encapsulating almost all the departments in one person. A partner is required to be a strategist, leader, manager, team-builder, work-winner, work do-er, financial controller, debt-collector, and compliance officer. A partner's skills are required to range from the visionary, through practical management, while at the same time focusing on the micro-detail of obscure areas of law. Chapter five, by Pippa Blakemore at The Pep Partnership, analyses three key categories – the strategic skills required, the business management techniques necessary to underpin the strategy, and the personal characteristics required to fulfil this multiplicity of responsibilities. Strategically, a partner is required to evaluate objectively where the firm, department and practice areas are now, where they want to be, and how to get there. Managerially, while trying to achieve the firm's vision and implement its mission, a partner is also expected to manage on a daily basis: clients, cases, matters, the firm and individuals. Personally, to achieve those expectations, a partner is required to have many individual qualities, which are fundamentally based on self-discipline, self-awareness and self-control. This chapter identifies the core traits required to be a partner, gives examples of when to use them, tips on how to implement, the benefits and why they are important.

Paul Williams, of Shook Hardy Bacon, looks at relationship-building in chapter six. How many times have you heard someone say, "It's not what you know, but who you know?" Sounds simple enough, but let's break it down. What you know matters a lot because unless you are knowledgeable and effective in your field and win the results that clients require, you will not become the "trusted advisor" that clients call when they need help, no matter who you know. Junior lawyers are confronted from the beginning of their career with the reality that what will set them apart from another is the time invested in studying and the effort invested in doing that accumulates experience and propels professional growth during their career. Junior attorneys generally learn to do this "what you know" part of the equation quite well. But, as these lawyers mature in the practice, they raise their heads and see that they are surrounded by other talented lawyers that have also worked hard and invested in professional development, each of them also winning the opportunity to play on our ultra-competitive playing field. So how does a client select a "trusted advisor" from this deep bench of talented attorneys? At this crucial moment, having established oneself as a capable competitor who can get the job done, "Who you know" now matters a lot. And who you have cultivated and developed a meaningful relationship with matters the most. Relationships are made over time. They require work and constant attention. And relationships must be year round, not only at holidays and times when they are convenient. Authentic relationships are especially fun, and they don't feel at all like work. In this chapter, Paul argues there is no one-size-fits-all instruction guide for building relationships. But, junior attorneys can absorb tips from mentors and employ these suggestions in their practice to develop their individual approach to creating meaningful relationships that will last a career and a lifetime.

Returning to Pippa, we look at the importance of relationships. The ability to create, build and maintain meaningful relationships is vital for a successful partner to provide excellent legal services. Relationships have always been an essential aspect of being a good lawyer, but the increasing use and impact of AI makes strong personal relationships even more important. Relationships progress from like, to trust, to entrust. Chapter seven identifies with whom attorneys should build relationships, including with clients, referrers, intermediaries and across the firm. There are a wide range of ideas on where and how to do this, including creative suggestions on networking, initiating a dialogue and ways in which to build rapport. It's important to make the most of the time invested, deciding how often to be in touch, which methods and what content are appropriate. And finally, how to turn contacts into clients and consistently meet those client expectations, so that partners turn them into their ambassadors. Many lawyers find these structured ideas abhorrent. They say, "I did not become a lawyer to be a salesperson". However, if a partner is an excellent lawyer, supported by an outstanding team, within a superlative firm, then that partner is letting down all the people the partner knows and meets, if that partner does not ensure that they and their firm help others in their time of legal need.

In chapter eight, Tom Bird looks at business development (BD). It is rare for a partnership to make someone up to partner who does not have the potential to be a work winner for the practice. Therefore, new partners will need to commit to building and developing a client portfolio. What should associates do now that will begin to develop and progress a pipeline of opportunities? Building on the relationship focus of chapters six and seven, Tom looks at the personal priorities that guarantee long-term business development success, as well as the role that confidence and curiosity can play in helping an associate develop quickly in this important area. The chapter explores what it is that highly effective work winners do to guarantee success and the specific relationship you are seeking to create with prospective clients. You will find that it is easier than you think.

Partners are expected to contribute to the financial success of the firm, which may include investing capital, sharing profits, and taking on financial risk. Therefore, lawyers seeking partnership should have a solid understanding of the financial aspects of partnership and be prepared to make a financial commitment to the firm.

In chapter nine, the first of two on financial management, Tony Young and Hung Tran of BDO, ask:

- Does the partner understand the drivers of the firm?
- Does the firm have strong discipline in managing these areas?
- Are there policies around the distribution of profits?
- What are the firm's prospects for growth?
- Is there rigor around the management of succession with senior partners?
- Does the firm have a reliance on particular industries or clients?

Nicky Owen of Crowe UK LLP then looks at the risk and the reward of becoming partner, and what people need to know and understand to be able to ask intelligent questions of management. In this chapter, Nicky provides solid examples of how partners can expect to see their finances change, highlighting in particular the UK experience.

The transition from employed to self-employed partner is a change in mindset in so many ways. Having insight into how you will be taxed helps you to understand your finances and how to manage them. In chapter 11, Nicky looks at:

- How will you be taxed?
- When will you receive your profit share?
- What happens to your benefits in kind?
- What is the basis of taxation?
- What is "Basis Period Reform" and how does this affect you?
- What's the difference between accounting profit and taxable profit, and why?

Finally, chapter 12 looks at wellbeing and partnership in law firms. Jean-Baptiste Lebelle, head of HR at Allen & Overy, explains that the concept of wellbeing in law firms has evolved significantly in recent years, as the legal profession faces increasing challenges of stress, burnout, mental health issues, and ethical dilemmas. Traditionally, wellbeing in law firms was largely ignored or equated with financial success, productivity, and reputation, often at the expense of personal health, happiness, and values. However, a growing body of research, advocacy, and best practices has highlighted the importance of fostering a culture of wellbeing in law firms especially since the COVID-19 pandemic. This major event has posed unprecedented challenges and disruptions to the legal profession, affecting the mental and physical health, productivity, and morale of lawyers. Therefore, every law firm should put wellbeing at the heart of their people strategy, especially for partners.

By implementing a true wellbeing strategy for partners, it can not only improve their own wellbeing, but also create a positive ripple effect and partners can be seen as role model for their peers, associates, clients, and the legal profession. Wellbeing and partnership status are not only compatible, but also complementary and beneficial for all stakeholders. Furthermore, wellbeing is now widely seen as essential for the success and sustainability of law firms, as it affects the quality and quantity of the work, the health and happiness of the lawyers, and the reputation and profitability of the firm.

About the authors

Tom Bird is a bestselling business author, trainer and keynote speaker who works internationally and specialises in all aspects of influence, selling, business development and presenting with a specific focus on professional service firms and international corporations. He has been designing and delivering training, writing business books, and speaking at conferences since 2001 and prior to that had a 12-year career in a number of sales and business leadership roles, including sales director of Northern Europe and vice president of European operations for both US and European based hi-tech companies. These roles gave Tom significant practical consultative selling, leadership, and business development experience and a real credibility and empathy with participants and the challenges they face in their daily roles and in how they approach winning work and developing client relationships.

Pippa Blakemore has worked for, advised, or presented to more than 400 law firms all over the world, ranging from international and national to small local firms, in many countries and across five continents. Pippa advises on key aspects of making law firms more successful, including strategy, leadership, management, teambuilding, business development, marketing, and public relations. She works in a range of capacities including as interim director of business development, head of marketing, project-specific work, ad hoc consultancy, presentations, seminars, training, and coaching. Pippa is a Freeman of the City of London.

Drawing on more than 20 years of talent development and human resources experience, **Jennifer Bluestein** leads all talent strategy and human resources functions at Perkins Coie. This includes associate, counsel, and staff recruitment, development and training, performance management, employee relations, compliance, compensation, and benefits. Jennifer deftly managed low attrition during the COVID-19 pandemic and implemented innovative wellbeing programming. With a focus on scaling a large talent organization to ensure strategic talent development on both the business professionals and legal sides of the firm, she has changed the evaluation and compensation process for associates as well as implementing the role of talent advisor and strategic workforce planning within the firm. Jennifer is passionate about making law firms a better place for everyone, but particularly for women, racial and ethnic minorities, and LGBTQ+ individuals. She was an integral part of the firm's leadership during the pandemic, responding to and anticipating the many day-to-day challenges the firm faced with a fully remote workforce.

Jean-Baptiste Lebelle is the HR director of Allen & Overy's Paris office. He holds a law degree from Paris II Assas and graduated from Sciences Po Paris. Jean-Baptiste taught at the Sorbonne and HEC on recruitment, retention, and career management in law firms. Jean-Baptiste has over 20 years of HR experience in the consulting sector and is especially engaged in topics related to compensation policies, recruitment, talent retention, diversity and inclusion, and wellbeing applied to law firms. He switched from headhunting for law firms to HR, becoming PWC Legal's HR director for Paris before A&O. Jean-Baptiste has contributed to several books produced for the International Bar Association by Globe Law & Business.

Nicky Owen heads up the professional practices team at Crowe UK LLP, delivering tax advice to firms and partners alike, covering a broad and in-depth spectrum. Nicky's clients are predominately within the professional practices and include lawyers from across a variety of firms. She loves working with people, partners, managing, and finance people in firms and team members, coming up with practical solutions that work. Nicky is passionate about what she does and wants to make it simple to understand, relevant, and non-technical. To achieve this, Nicky draws from her in-depth knowledge and experience gained over 30 years. Nicky is a people person and is an ally to the various ED&I networks within Crowe.

David Parnell is the founder of True North Partner Placement, a legal recruitment boutique. Along with over two decades of experience in the legal recruitment industry, he is also an author (ABA Publishing and Ark Group), speaker, *American Lawyer* research fellow and former media contributor (Forbes and American Lawyer Media). David's work can also be found in the likes of *Inc.*, *The Huffington Post*, *Venture Capital Post*, *Fox News Magazine*, *Lawyerist*, *Australasian Lawyer*, *NBC News*, *National Law Journal*, *Law360*, *Bloomberg*, *Legal Business World*, *The Global Legal Post*, *Business Insider*, *NZ Lawyer*, *ABA Journal* and *The Bleacher Report*, among others.

Claire Rason is a consultant, podcaster, and accredited individual and team coach. She founded Client Talk (a coaching-powered consultancy) to help firms enhance their relationships both inside the firm, as well as externally with clients. Claire is skilled at creating business and client development strategies for professional services companies alongside the provision of the training and coaching needed to bring these to life. However, what sets her apart is her understanding of the psychology that sits behind all of this. She works with professionals to help them communicate better, whilst embracing change and challenge. She is passionate about seeing more parity in professional services firms and works with firms to create systemic change.

Michael Roster was formerly managing partner of Morrison & Foerster's Los Angeles office, co-chair of the firm's financial institutions practice group worldwide, and a member of the firm's policy committee. In 1993, Michael was appointed general counsel of Stanford University, Stanford Medical Center, and Stanford Management Company. He subsequently was executive vice president and general counsel of Golden West Financial Corporation. Michael has also served as chair of the Association of Corporate Counsel, chair of the Stanford Alumni Association, steering committee co-chair of ACC's Value Challenge, and chair of two start-up companies. He currently teaches Contract Drafting and Analysis at the University of Southern California Gould School of Law and is a director of MDRC in New York, a non-profit organization that evaluates the effectiveness of government and other programs affecting lower- and moderate-income families and individuals.

Hung Tran is a business services partner with BDO in Brisbane. His strengths include understanding his clients' needs and building trust to ensure the desired outcome is achieved. Hung provides individuals and companies with business and taxation advice, including guidance on business structuring, succession planning, and how to effectively handle the ongoing management of a business to ensure goals are achieved. He also provides an outsourced finance function to many of his clients. Hung joined BDO in 2004 and became partner in July 2010. With a specialisation in building, construction, and property management, he leads the firm's real estate and construction sector team.

Paul Williams is the managing partner for Shook, Hardy & Bacon's Denver office and the co-chair of the firm's general liability litigation practice group. He is also on the firm's executive committee. Paul partners with clients to create relationships that achieve better legal outcomes. He believes win-win partnerships with clients are built on collaboration, innovation, strategic action, and trust – all of which ultimately bring better results and the metrics to prove them. Paul has been named a Client Service All-Star by BTI Consulting for his client-first-focused relationships. *Best Lawyers in America*, *National Law Journal*, *Benchmark Litigation*, *Who's Who Legal* and *Chambers USA* have all recognized Paul based on his legal success and client input. Paul is a featured speaker, panelist, author, and resource for publications and organizations including *The American Lawyer*, the American Bar Association and the Association of Corporate Counsel.

Tony Young is a partner in the business services division at BDO. With over 40 years in the chartered accounting profession, Tony brings impressive experience providing taxation and commercial advice to a diverse selection of clients, including professionals, property developers, manufacturers, and retailers. Tony deals with clients from wide-ranging backgrounds, particularly family-owned and operated businesses. He also provides strategic advice to professional service firms who are looking to grow their business.

Chapter 1:
What does "partner" even mean?

By Michael Roster, former managing partner, Morrison & Foerster's Los Angeles office

There are lots of reasons for a lawyer to aim for partnership at a law firm, no matter its size. First, it is an important lifetime credential, somewhat like tenure at an educational institution. It says that this lawyer has met a high standard in her or his profession. If said lawyer goes off to do other things and then wishes to return to a law firm, the transition becomes much easier because their resume says they previously achieved partner status.

Second, as a partner you can have a much more significant role in shaping how your practice group and your department function, as well as the firm overall. Depending on the governance structures at your firm, how much latitude you have – especially as a new partner – can vary widely. At some firms, even senior partners have little say in the firm's governance. But at other firms, even large ones, junior partners are often encouraged to take leading roles, and early on. Among other things, this helps build newer and fresher perspectives into the firm. It helps junior partners develop strong management skills, now and for the future. It also signals to clients that the firm is young and dynamic. Even if you only take a secondary, deputy-type role in leading your practice group or department as well as on firm-wide committees, if you do your homework and become trusted by your colleagues, you can have a major impact on decision-making. It puts you in line someday to play an even more significant role at the firm.

Third, becoming a partner at your firm can give you better standing if you later wish to go in-house or move into a non-legal position. In interviews, it demonstrates that you already meet high professional standards. If you become an in-house lawyer, what your law firm providers are doing for your company is not a mystery, as it can be for other in-house lawyers who have never been at a law firm, or if they have, not as partners. Having been a partner, you understand the economics and other dynamics of your law firm providers. As a result, you are more skilled at selecting and then managing those outside service providers.

Some economic factors

It is worth keeping in mind some of the economic risks and challenges of becoming a law firm partner. These will be explained in more detail in chapters nine and ten but a brief overview is provided here. The most important issue is that you, as a partner, can now be personally liable if anything should go wrong at the firm. Yes, most law firms now operate as LLCs or in similar capacities and carry professional liability insurance, but the risks are still there. Even in an LLC, many landlords and banks may require personal guarantees from individual partners. You should also keep in mind that the income streams you depend upon as a partner, including for work already done, may be diverted to pay creditors and others. That's not a risk you had when you were an associate.

When you become a partner, you also will be expected to contribute capital – often a smaller amount in the first year but with increasing amounts depending on your share of the firm's equity and/or how long you've been a partner. Assuming you don't have the amount of cash that will be required, you will need to borrow some or all of the capital that is required upfront and then ongoing in future years. Those loans will carry interest, and at increasing rates if market interest rates rise.

Keep in mind, if you later leave the firm, you usually won't get that capital back for a while – sometimes quite a while. Some firms have extended the return of capital from what once was a matter of months to a matter of years, possibly five or even ten years. So you will be paying interest on your capital loans even though you are no longer at the firm. It is therefore important for you to carefully read the capital loan documents, as some lenders may accelerate your payments if you withdraw from the firm. And if your former law firm later has problems, you may never see that capital but will still need to pay off the principal and interest on the bank loans for which you are responsible. It also is important for you to read the partnership agreement's provisions regarding the return of capital, including the choice of law provisions that may work against you. Some firms may repay your capital by transferring accounts receivable to you for matters for which you were the responsible partner. In practice, some withdrawing partners will have considerable difficulty in recovering their capital.

This issue becomes even more complicated if you move to a new law firm instead of going in-house or pursuing other career options, because your new law firm will also expect capital upfront, and then usually more capital as time goes on. So now you may have loans for your capital requirements at two law firms.

During bad economic times in the past, some firms even went to their non-equity partners and demanded capital from them as a condition for their remaining at the firms, albeit as non-equity partners.

No matter what the LLC or other corporate structure, if your firm has financial shortfalls, there will likely be additional capital calls on you. Meaning, either you will have the cash for the increased capital call or you will need to borrow still more, and if the capital call is the result of economic troubles nationally or worldwide, your ability to obtain still more personal loans becomes more difficult than during good economic times, and definitely more costly.

Many, if not most, law firms actually operate at a loss until the last two or three months of the firm's fiscal year. That's because they typically pay out as much as possible to their existing partners at year-end since the partners are going to be taxed on the full income booked by the firm. That's the reason for all of those emails and telephone calls by partners to their clients at year-end, urging clients to pay the firm's bills as fast as possible. But that means the pipeline for cash flow is largely exhausted by the collection efforts, even though the firm will still have all of its regular obligations in subsequent months, such as for payroll and the benefits of its salaried workers, including associates, rent, utilities, and similar obligations. Which usually means, on top of the personal loans you may have taken, your firm itself may have taken loans for its ongoing operations. This is in addition to loans your firm may have obtained for improvements to its office space, for equipment it may have purchased instead of leased, and so on.

You also now have to pay for your own health, retirement, and other benefits (and at many firms, even your office furniture), all of which can take a sizeable percentage from what once was your salary. In other words, when you are told a junior partner made $X amount last year, that's before that junior partner had to pay for items that she or he didn't have to pay personally when an associate.

If your law firm operates in numerous states or countries, you are likely going to have to file tax returns in each of those jurisdictions. Most multi-jurisdiction law firms will file partnership-wide returns in each jurisdiction and will provide each partner with information regarding their individual income and tax numbers. This adds substantial complexity to your tax filings, including the need to allocate your income for different jurisdictions and as offset by the taxes you paid elsewhere – all of which is subject to audit by the numerous jurisdictions. In some instances, you may be required to pay taxes in a foreign jurisdiction but may not be able to offset those taxes against the tax obligations of your home jurisdiction, which means that in some instances you could be double taxed on your foreign jurisdiction income. If you have not already done so as an associate, it is highly likely that you will need to retain an accountant to assist you in preparing your personal income taxes.

Doing excellent legal work matters – a lot

Assuming you are on track to become a partner, this typically means you already have demonstrated the professional and other skills that the firm seeks in its partners. But that doesn't mean you can slack off. Quite the contrary. The quality of your legal work matters and is usually the primary factor in deciding each year which associates and counsel might be invited to join the partnership, and as you progress in your legal career, even as a partner, the firm will expect your legal skill to progress as well.

Some firms elevate candidates to partnership across the board and without predetermined categories. But that will usually mean there is a committee or similar group, often from multiple practice groups and offices, that will meet and discuss whether each candidate meets the high expectations that the firm has for moving a lawyer from associate or of-counsel to partner status.

Other firms limit the number of partners based on allocations. These allocations might be based on the revenues, profitability, or size of a given office, practice group, or department, or maybe a combination of these factors. Some firms also want to maintain a predetermined ratio of partners to associates, among other things, so their "profits per partner" numbers at the American Lawyer and elsewhere look good. And so now allocating partner slots becomes an allocation of a scarce resource, and once again, the quality of your work will typically be the most important factor, or at least one of the two or three most important factors.

What are the other factors? Depending on the firm, they might include:

- Hours billed, year after year.
- Client satisfaction, based on informal feedback through the years, or possibly specific calls to clients asking for such feedback.
- Client development, meaning how helpful you have been in attracting and then retaining clients, and in some cases, whether you have established the primary relationship with one or more clients.
- Quality of participation in practice group, department, and firmwide activities such as recruiting, training, and mentoring.
- Participation in bar association and similar activities.

- Conformity with the firm's culture.
- Diversity.

Input for these factors is usually based on evaluations from your specific practice group, but is also often based on observations from people throughout the firm.

Most firms expect new partners to build on their legal and other skills as well as their books of business in the years following admission to the partnership. You may also want to keep in mind those four standard descriptors of what lawyers do – finder, minder, binder, and grinder. And here, some firms don't give especially high credit to candidates who might be considered "servicing partners" – that is, partners who turn out high-quality work for clients, day after day and year after year, but do little if any client generation. The reality is that a servicing partner's billing rate will likely increase each year, with the risk that, over time, junior lawyers will be able to turn out that same high-quality work but at lower billing rates. This is why servicing partners are at greater risk of being "de-equitized" or even counseled out of the firm altogether, particularly in bad financial times.

In that regard, I remember a breakfast years ago where ten to 15 general counsel had gathered from what might best be described as trophy clients – that is, clients that firms love to name as part of their client base. We were going to be on panels throughout the day but had decided to convene for breakfast in order to share our recent experiences and war stories. The name of a law firm and a specific partner somehow came up in the discussion, whereupon we heard that the partner might be leaving the firm because the firm considered him solely a servicing partner. It turned out virtually every general counsel at the table knew this partner and highly valued that partner's work. The fact that every one of our companies was using this partner and valued him so highly is something we then realized that the law firm's senior management might not even take into account, absent our telling the firm how important that partner was to our relationship with the firm. Which several of us did, and the partner remained.

Time to partnership

Some firms are explicit about the time to partnership, whilst some have ranges of time when a person will first be considered, and some keep it entirely undefined. Some firms remain fixated on ratios (for example, four associates per partner and including firmwide, by office, and by specific department/practice group). Some firms have created intermediate landing spots (of-counsel, senior counsel, non-equity partner, etc.).

At my original law firm, associates were elevated to partner status within five to six years and we all then rose, lockstep, in the course of eight to 12 years, to the same ultimate share of the firm as its founders. Very few firms have retained this lockstep approach, although one advantage was that we would never make someone a partner unless we felt for a certainty that they deserved not only to be a partner, but over time would be at the highest ranks in the firm.

In recent years, I've met one-on-one or in groups with law firm chairs and managing partners and have advocated that their firms return to a system when associates would become partners after, say, five or six years. As a former chair at Morrison & Foerster used to say, we know within a few years which associates can meet our high standards or else they shouldn't be with us in the first place. We have them doing multi-million dollar, even multi-billion-dollar, deals for our clients, so we should want them also to care about their own futures and thus whether they would even want to be partners at our firm. As a result, we distributed economic data to the associates and tried to instill in them the idea that this was their future.

I also remember doing a retreat several years ago at a very strong super-regional law firm. I met in the morning with the firm's partners to discuss changes in the legal environment, including reasons to return to fixed prices, retainers and the like. I was then taken to the firm's large meeting room where the associates had been assembled in person and remotely. The chair told the associates that the partners had met with me all morning, but that didn't matter as much as what would be accomplished at lunch with the associates. As the chair told the gathered associates, "You are what the firm is and is going to be. You are the ones to decide how this firm will function in the future. And thus these are important issues for you to consider, and possibly more so than for the current partners." The firm's chairman then said he was going to leave the room in order to assure a truly open and robust discussion.

I gave a short presentation but then spent most of the time answering questions from the associates. The questions were extraordinary, and I could readily see that these associates had long ago considered the firm as theirs, and in turn, their future. By the way, most of the associates made partner at this firm, and a very large percent spent their entire legal careers there.

Your clients are both outside and inside the firm

Some firms look at whether an associate being considered for partnership has already developed client relationships and a book of business.

Whether or not this is a factor at your law firm, as an associate you should want to start developing relationships with your peers who are in-house – both those with whom you are working on client matters and those with whom you otherwise have gotten to know as a result of bar association functions, alumni gatherings and the like. Someday, those peers are going to be general counsel and deputy general counsel of your clients and prospective clients. You and they are going to advance in your careers largely in parallel, and in fact, you will find you develop very strong and long-lasting professional and social relationships with these colleagues.

It's also useful to treat the other partners and associates at your firm as your clients. That is, you are doing work for and with them, and they in turn are evaluating you – consciously or unconsciously – in much the same way as your actual clients are evaluating you. If you keep this interrelationship in mind, without trying to be manipulative about it, you will find it can greatly enhance how you are evaluated at the time you are considered for partnership.

Business development and relationship building will be covered in detail in chapters six, seven and eight.

Some personal factors

Be sure your spouse, partner, family, and friends understand that being a partner doesn't mean you will work less, that you will no longer be working late and on weekends, or that you and your family will no longer need to reschedule long-planned vacations. You still have the same clients who have the same demands upon you and your firm, only now you also are being evaluated on the retention and profitability of those clients as well as the productivity of all the other professionals who you supervise.

At many law firms, partners actually bill more hours than associates, not necessarily because the partners want to achieve high hourly targets (although they also know how many hours they bill can often affect what levels of payouts they are awarded year-to-year), but because that's what you need to do to keep your clients happy.

Client development also becomes a higher priority. Some firms consider all clients to be clients of the firm, whereas other firms keep track of who first created a client relationship and award origination credits to that partner, year after year, even if the partner who first brought in work from the client now does little if any work for that client and even if you are the one largely handling the client's work. Many firms also evaluate how large your book of business might be when deciding your share of the firm's profits.

Depending on the firm, your compensation may be substantially linked to these factors, but with other partners typically wanting credit for the same clients and the same billings. A former chair at Morrison & Foerster used to joke (and it was only a partial joke) that if we had the client billings that each partner had claimed for herself or himself, we'd have multiple times the profits than was the case.

In recent decades, the ability of partners to move laterally to other firms has become much more common. Whereas in the past, partners often spent their entire careers at a single firm, today some partners may make a number of lateral moves. In many, if not most, cases, the moving partner's portable book of business is the most critical factor in their ability to move and the compensation they will receive at their new firm. This has had a significant impact on law firm cultures and – at least to many clients and partners – can be very negative.

In conclusion

Becoming a law firm partner is a very worthwhile goal. It is a real achievement in your career and in your life and can be enormously gratifying. It says all of those costs of law school and all of that time spent as an associate have given you rare status among your fellow professionals. But law firm partnership also has its risks and its costs. It is not for everyone. Be sure you have considered all of this before you sign that partnership agreement.

Chapter 2: So you want to make partner? Evaluating your firm's partnership prospects

By David Parnell, founder of True North Partner Placement

Introduction

Over 20-plus years of legal recruitment I've heard countless variations of "I want to make partner". As you might imagine, some were more believable than others. Many-to-most of them were sincere. At least I believed that they believed they were sincere. But, unless you consider "I'll bill a ton of hours" a quality partner-bound plan – which I don't – it was a distinct minority that had developed a basic plan, much less a quality strategy, for accomplishing it. And absent a plan or strategy for rising to the occasion, were they really serious about it? This brings us to you, the reader.

Assuming you're (a) a mere mortal and (b) *truly* serious about making partner, there are a host of things you can and should do/create to increase your chances – a strategy, proper business development, marketing, brand-building and networking plans and execution, to name several. We'll cover none of those here. What we will address is an extremely important part of the equation – an assessment of your environment (demographics, practice composition, firm-based financials, etc.) to see if your current firm provides fertile ground for achieving and maintaining partnership.

In my original draft of this writing, I used the term "the highest statistical probability" in place of "fertile ground". I switched to the latter, however, because the former was a bit too concise. We're not drawing this down to a specific number – 37 percent or 52 percent, for instance – because we can't. To the best of my knowledge, there exists no algorithm for partnership probability. But, by generating, aggregating, and comparing/contrasting some logically relevant data, observations, and anecdotes, you can become significantly more conscious and explicit about the path you're on, and make stronger decisions about what is "better" vs "worse" for making partner, thus giving you more control over your own destiny. So, what does this look like?

Well, we might start by asking, "What are the attributes that can/will better predispose you to making partner?" Or, otherwise stated, what does the "ground" look like that is fertile for partnership? To answer that, we might consider how one actually makes partner at a law firm. And no, it isn't a function of simply taking on all of the hours that happen to arrive at your doorstep and "doing a good job". Yes, partners do like that; it makes them money. But that is just the price of admission. Unless you're at one of the elite firms that focuses on institutional clients and whose brand draws in the business (a statistical outlier that represents a sliver of the law firm population) there is much more to the "making partner" equation. At 5,000 ft, this might look something like:

- Business development (generating revenue that financially justifies your presence);
- Excel at being an asset to the firm while you develop said business (bill substantial hours at high rates while requiring little-to-no hand holding); and
- Networking and politicking (wooing the right partners while avoiding annoying the wrong ones).

In other words, at least get started on the track of independently making the firm enough money to support all of your expenses, bill a lot of hours while performing quality work, and make friends in the process. Accomplishing these requires something along the lines of:

- Developing a marketable skill set (a function of quality and quantity of work and exposure to the right types of clients and opportunities);
- Developing and executing on marketing and brand-building efforts (conferences, external networking, writing/content generation, etc.); and
- Sales (internal and external – getting in front of the right partners and potential clients and developing relationships and formally or informally signing them).

In other words, getting invited to the right jobs and parties and having enough time and talent to accomplish these extracurricular activities. Along with some luck, accomplishing these is made much easier in a firm that:

- Has a sellable brand, with some level of flexibility in billing and client intake and is actively engaging in quality work with quality clients;

- Has your practice area with a critical mass and level of influence within the firm; and
- Offers you low direct competition, and demographics that are conducive to, and show a track record of, bringing in and up, junior partners.

Even though all of that is a mouthful, it's not comprehensive. But, at a higher level, the reasoning tracks – at least in my book – and leaves one to consider a particular battery of criteria/attributes when gauging a firm's propensity for making partners. But first, let's address some points that are necessary to understand, process, and therefore accept, the content that follows.

Assumptions / disclaimers / expectations / axioms

We will speak (very) often in generalizations. For instance, developing a book of business that covers your expenses and puts profit into the firm's pool will *generally* make you a partner. But is this always the case? No. There are exceptions. This brings us to an axiom: Exceptions prove the rule. This isn't a physics course. We aren't working in absolutes here.

Some of the points we address may not be relevant for your practice. For example, very small practices like tax controversy or appellate work will have a relatively small stable of partners – perhaps only one – making it difficult to find/determine trendlines. I encourage you to extract what is relevant and ignore the rest.

Black and white vs gray. Your goal for evaluating a firm – your current or a lateral target – should be to make the "most educated guess" as opposed to arriving at a digital "yes" or "no". While it's possible that, having read through this, you'll see your target firm as an obvious "yes" or "no", you should expect shades of gray.

While junior associates can definitely benefit from this, because the partnership-bid calculus shifts with age, those that will benefit most from the following information are at mid-career and above.

The social aspects of the partner-making process are exceedingly important and include rapport, cultural integration, and loyalty. These are important things to consider, too, when governing/directing your own behavior and when evaluating your competition. But due to the complexity of their nature, we won't address them here.

Firms are profit centers. So, one greatly increases one's chances of partnership by making the process a profitability play. To be direct, law firms are capitalistic in nature. So, generally speaking, if you are autonomously profitable, then you're in. Are there exceptions? Sure. But without more context, this is an axiom. Exception to the profitability play: firms that primarily feed off institutional clients. This is a different animal as, generally, business development isn't required – it may even be frowned upon. Along with a brutal work ethic and exquisite product, making partner at one of these firms will be more a function of networking and politicking (both are expansive and complex subjects).

Since we are operating in a highly complex and shifting environment where we will never even approach making a 100 percent, wholly informed decision, unless otherwise stated, we are lending credence to, and therefore looking for, track records of certain behaviors (i.e., histories). This is because, on the whole, track records are anecdotally, if not statistically, more predictive of future behavior. For example, some might argue that if a firm hasn't made a partner in ten years, it is bound to make one soon. That said, my money is on the firm that has made a partner every year for the last ten years. We can blame this choice jointly and severally on mathematics (Pareto's principle) and/or physics (inertia vs momentum) and/or economics (the Lindy Effect), among other things.

While you are (at least for the moment) solely focusing on your own firm (and whatever data you can extract from it), much of the criteria can/will be more accurate if related to peer firms (e.g., firms that match in multiple areas of size, internationality, financials, practice portfolio composition, domestic footprint, etc.)

Evaluate your readiness first

While your firm's propensity/fitness toward making you (or others) partner is important, it won't matter if your own house isn't in order. I encourage you to place yourself under a microscope. Making partner is not a one-sided street, of course, and you will need to go to great lengths to achieve it, even in the friendliest environment. With that in mind, I ask you, are you ready and willing? Are you doing all of the things necessary to make partner? Do you know what they are? When you consider the partners that you work for, are you doing all of the same things they did to earn their positions? If you are, how do you know that? Are you assuming that or did you discuss with them the path they took? There is much to consider. Below are some points to get you started:

- Have you spent some time formally evaluating and considering the lifestyle of the younger partners at your firm? Be honest with yourself

– is it something that you want to inherit? Or are you primarily driven by other things, like money, prestige, impressing others? Like a tattoo, this is (kind of) forever. Make sure that you love it.

- Do you have a granular, articulated strategy for making partner? Does it (at least) include (a) a business plan, (b) a marketing plan, (c) a brand-building plan, (d) a networking plan, (e) a skillset-building plan, and (f) a map for executing them?
- If you're relatively senior, have you begun trying to build some business? Have you at least begun setting up potential business-building relationships? How about sales pitches? Are you at least seeking to be a part of pitch teams?
- Do you have a formal mentorship with a partner that is a power center in the firm (or, are they at least power adjacent)?
- How often are you networking with other partners in your group? In the firm?
- Where marketing is concerned, a rule of thumb is to go deep, then broad. So, have you begun efforts to develop a name (a brand) in some narrow and profitable area of law? Are you now, or are you at least on your way to being, considered an expert in some niche? This can be a key ingredient to your eventual marketability.
- How familiar are you with your firm's governance and policies and procedures? Specifically, do you understand your firm's policies regarding financial hygiene and client intake standards? Do you understand (at least at a higher level) law firm economics?
- How crisp/clean is your own financial hygiene? Do you hand in your timesheets/billing on time? Are you involved in collections in some way, shape, or form?

Evaluate your firm's readiness

I'd be surprised if you've deployed *all* of these, but they are staple criteria/actions that should be in line at some point between mid- and late-associate status. With those addressed, let's turn to evaluating your firm. We'll start with the most basic and obvious – do you have any competition?

Your competition

Associates

Quantity. How many other associates are you competing against? While having little-to-no competition isn't necessarily a good thing – a lack of competition may be due to a slowly dying practice, for instance – generally speaking, the fewer you have the better. From an assessment standpoint, this should be low hanging fruit, too. If your group is sprawling, you may need to do a bit more leg work, but for all intents and purposes, a quick look at your group on the firm's website will be sufficient.

Quality. This is a much more complicated, multifaceted measuring stick, but I'd be remiss if I didn't mention it. Of course, much of this is subjective – their "likeability", your perception of how they are perceived by the partners, your perception of their relationships with others in the group, etc. Some of it is objective, however – their "go-to" status among the partners, their hours, their placement on, and leadership of, teams, etc. Some things to consider:

- Do you have a window into what actions they are taking toward making partner? If so, are they more advanced/comprehensive/professionally executed than your strategy so far?
- Do they, to your knowledge, have a head start on one or more of the other "readiness" factors that I've addressed above? Perhaps they've come up during conversation?
- Do they seem to be better liked by the partners inside and/or outside of your practice (as is evidenced by frequent, warm interactions)?
- Do they have any personal/social relationships with partners and/or leadership? Particularly, do these transcend work boundaries?
- Do they consistently get deal/matter lead spots instead of you?
- Do they consistently get offered more hours than you? Do they consistently bill more hours than you?
- Is the level of responsibility/work that they are given more appealing than yours?
- What do their credentials look like compared to yours? Law school pedigree and academic accolades (grades, scholarships, law review, moot court, etc.)?

- Do they now, or have they in the past, brought in business and/or client relationships?
- To the degree that your firm facilitates formal mentorships, do you perceive that their mentor/mentee relationship is stronger/better than yours?
- When considering the firm's political landscape, does their mentor seem to be a stronger power center and/or more power adjacent than yours?
- Are they brought on pitches while you are not?
- Do they have a "marketability" factor that you do not? (Clerkship, stint in government, etc.)
- How does their dress/fashion compare to yours? I know this may sound petty, but it can be a factor.
- How does their level of extroversion and social appeal compare to yours?

We could brainstorm to come up with many more considerations, but I think you get the picture. Determine your direct competition and then consider them through these lenses. How do you stack up? If some variation of "not good" is bubbling up, some changes will need to be made.

Partners

While this may be a bit premature, it won't hurt to consider who you might be competing against for business if/when you make partner. We'll talk about junior partners a bit later, but for now, if there are junior and/or more senior partners that are demonstrable rainmakers, how will you stack up against them? Will you be able to navigate around them in the market – e.g., pitch for work that they wouldn't be pursuing? And if you can't, will you be able to complement their skills in a way that they will bring you into pitches?

Of course, you'll need to make partner first for this to be a potential issue. But assuming that you do, the coronation is the start of the race, not the end. To be direct, the presence of younger partners is – or, at least should be – a very good sign. Like a still-singing canary in the coalmine, you'll want to see them in your firm. But it does make sense to consider how you'll navigate with/around them once you make it to the big leagues. Considering what the runway looks like post-ascension should occupy a spot in your algorithm.

Size of the practice

You'll want a practice that is materially sized, both (a) in relation to the market (i.e., same practice in other firms) and (b) in relation to other practices within your firm. Think, "How large is my practice in comparison to other firms' practices, and how large is my practice compared to other practices within my firm?"

Generally speaking, the larger the practice is (vis-à-vis its peers in other firms and to other practices within the firm itself) the more fertile and active the group will be both externally (acquiring business over competitors) and internally (acquiring time, capital, and resources within the firm). A 40-person group is more likely to attract resources and capital and see upward mobility than a 20-person group. We can blame this on the Pareto principle too. Further, the size of the practice in comparison to the rest of the firm can be informative. Usually, the more capital and real estate a group consumes/occupies, the more business it generates, and business generation directly correlates to influence, opportunity, and priority within a firm.

Of course, this will be relative. Considering the 40-person group above, for example: if they comprise ten percent of their firm's total make up, and the 20-person group comprises 30 percent, this moves the needle.

Proximity to power/influence

Often, making partner is equal parts performance and politics. Short of a book of business that is too large to ignore, you'll need to have the right people firmly in your corner. And what does "right" mean? In this case, people that are sources of power and influence in the firm.

Now, I realize that this sounds Machiavellian. That said, it is just plain true and you can disregard it at your own peril. So how might you recognize these people? Well, you might look for partners with formal leadership roles, large books of business, deep relationships with important clients, committee members – partnership and compensation, in particular – franchise-level brands/profiles in the marketplace, multiple third-party rankings, etc. Earning advocacy from the likes of these partners will carry significant weight when decision day comes. To help facilitate your ingratiation, you'll want to have access to as many as possible.

With that in mind, the size of the practice in your office compared to the rest of the group (domestically speaking) can be informative when considered through this lens. For example, who do you think will have more opportunities to build their network and otherwise engage in internal politics? Associate A, who is in a small satellite office where there are no partners from their group, or Associate B, who works out of the mothership, home to the majority of the group's partners? If you're Associate A, and the center of influence for your group (and maybe the firm as a whole) is generally inaccessible, this demands some evaluation.

That said, considering the 40- and 20-person groups we mentioned previously: what if the 40-person group only comprises ten percent of the firm's lawyers, but 90 percent of the group is situated in your office, which happens to be a satellite office? And what if only ten percent of the 20-person group is situated in your office, which is the mothership? You'll want to take a deeper look at this. Being near the majority of the group is generally more attractive than not. But a group that is isolated from the firm – sometimes an acquired group from another firm, for instance – may have no horsepower at all. Being located in the mothership where you can ingratiate yourself with numerous other power players deserves significant consideration, too, even if it doesn't host the majority of your group. For example, to the degree that there is a partnership committee, what is your proximity to the members? Are any of them a part of your practice? Are any in your office? Of course, the more the better.

Track record

Here, we're talking about (a) the overall movement/flow of associates into and through partnership and eventually into retirement, and (b) the relative linearity of partner maturity (ages). Of course, you'll want to see a track record of the firm having made partners, and ideally within your own group. And yes, there is an argument to be made for a firm that hasn't made a partner in a long time. Aren't they due? Well, maybe. But the more important question is, "Why haven't they made a partner in a long time?" Practices that are marketable, draw in business, and otherwise make more money for the firm are rarely stagnant.

Mind you, I said "practices", not "partners" – there should be a distinction. When considered as a profit center (in accounting parlance), a practice may be highly profitable. But said profit may derive (solely) from a single partner with a huge book of business. In this case, all of the attorneys may simply be tasked with servicing the book. This potentially is – and, in the case of a firm that hasn't made a partner in that group for a long time, definitely is – indicative of a group that has little-to-no appetite for making more partners. Might they be open to lateral partners with books? Sure, but that's a different story. Where you're concerned, a situation like this doesn't look good. The following are some points to consider.

Younger partners

How many younger partners does the firm have? How about within your respective group? What do I mean by "young", by the way? Well, I have no hard and fast parameters, but a good cohort might be partners in their mid-30s to mid-40s. You will at least want to see a material number of them among the firm's total partnership ranks. What does "material" mean? Again, that's relative.

Our database has ~220K attorneys and ~93K of them are partners. When we graph the age distribution of those partners, we get the distribution curve in Figure 1. The quantity of partners that (a) have a graduation date on their bio (which is the information we use to ascertain their assumed ages), and (b) fall within the age range of 32-80, is 91,907. We use the age of 32 as an absolute minimum, and derive that from the assumption that attorneys graduate from law school at the age of 24 and the average partnership track is still eight years. We're undershooting the age by ~1 year in some cases, and the partnership track continues to extend, but we're taking the conservative route.

That said, the number of partners that fall in the 32-45yrs cohort is 35,705. So, a good barometer for your firm's partnership ranks as a whole should be circa the 39 percent mark for "younger" partners. Ideally, you'd have one or more of them in your group. If that isn't the case, you'll want to know why.

Figure 1: Age distribution of partners.

Permanent attorney class

Permanent attorneys are senior associates or of-counsels that are no longer on the firm's normal partnership track. You'll want to know how many your firm has and what their ages are. If there are a lot of them, the firm may be a parking lot for associates that couldn't/didn't make partner. Talent incubation is expensive, so it's hard to let go. But too many permanent attorneys can be indicative of (a) a less-than aggressive attitude toward making partners, and/or (b) a less-than robust financial constitution among the group. Permanent class attorneys can get expensive, and clients are generally less willing to pay higher rates for non-partner billables. With that being the case, why wouldn't the firm turn those permanent attorneys into partners? That question can have many answers. But, to be direct, we don't (or at least shouldn't) really care why your firm is doing it. All that we need to know is that a larger than average pool of permanent attorneys detracts from your chances of making partner.

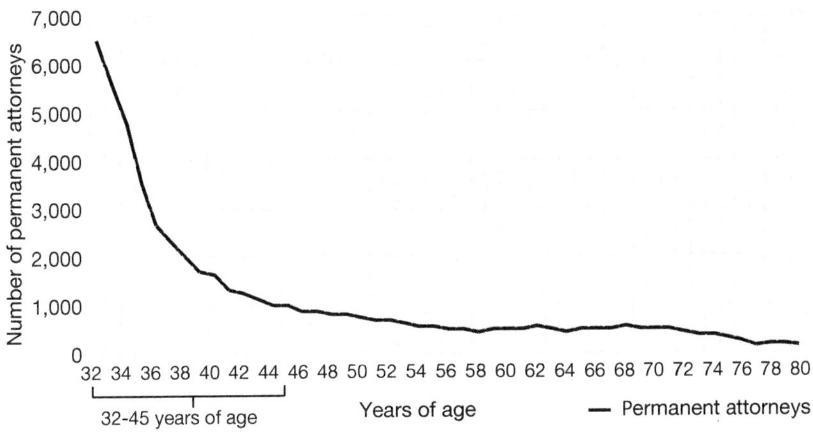

Figure 2: Age distribution of permanent attorneys.

At the time of writing, our DB has ~110K sub-partner-class attorneys (associates, "attorneys", and of-counsel). Of that ~110K, ~57.5K can be considered "permanent class" (they are >/= 32 years of age). So, the permanent class represents ~52% of the entire sub-partner-class.

Permanent class sub-group

Of the permanent class, ~37K are between the ages of 32 and 45. This sub-group comprises ~64 percent of the total permanent class. Of the 32-45-year-old sub-group, 32-36, 37-42 and 43-45 comprise 41 percent

(~23K attorneys),16 percent (~9K attorneys) and 6 percent (~3K attorneys), respectively. Looking at Figure 3, you can see that the 40-year-old mark is where the partner trend line starts to come down, i.e., firms are generally peaking in their appetite for partners, and we can make a strong presumption that they are converting fewer and fewer of those permanent attorneys.

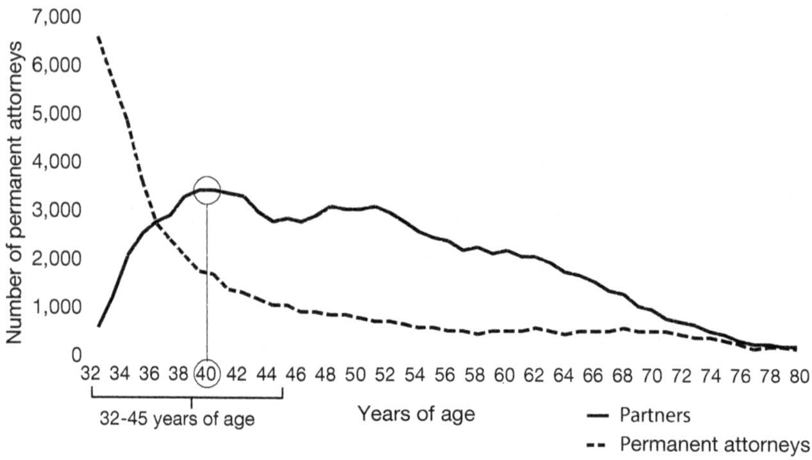

Figure 3: Age distribution of total attorneys.

Total permanent class constitution

To make this a bit easier on you from the perspective of information gathering and evaluation, let's use the entire sub-partner-class attorney values. At ~110k for the *total* sub-partner-class, we have the following (rough) benchmarks:

- ~21 percent between the ages of 32-36.
- ~Eight percent between the ages of 37-42.
- ~Three percent between the ages of 43-47.

Ideally, you would compare your group's constitution to those of peer firms in the market. Different practices have different profit/operation profiles, which can and will shift their constitutions. That said, the above figures offer a good barometer to work from. Ideally, your firm will have fewer permanent class attorneys than the given averages.

Distribution

Is there a relatively smooth, linear trend line without major gaps in the partners' ages? Is it top- heavy, bottom-heavy, or a barbell? As should be obvious, the more linear and comprehensive the age progression of the partnership is, the more likely it is to continue on in that direction.

While this can be considered at the firm, practice, and office levels, depending on the size of your practice, you may want to (need to) focus at the firm level. Appellate, for instance, likely won't have a large-enough stable of partners to effectively map, so the distribution may be spotty. Ideally, you'd understand what the firm considers a profit center – i.e., is it practice-oriented, office-oriented, or a mix of both – and, based on that, you could get a much more predictive pool to evaluate.

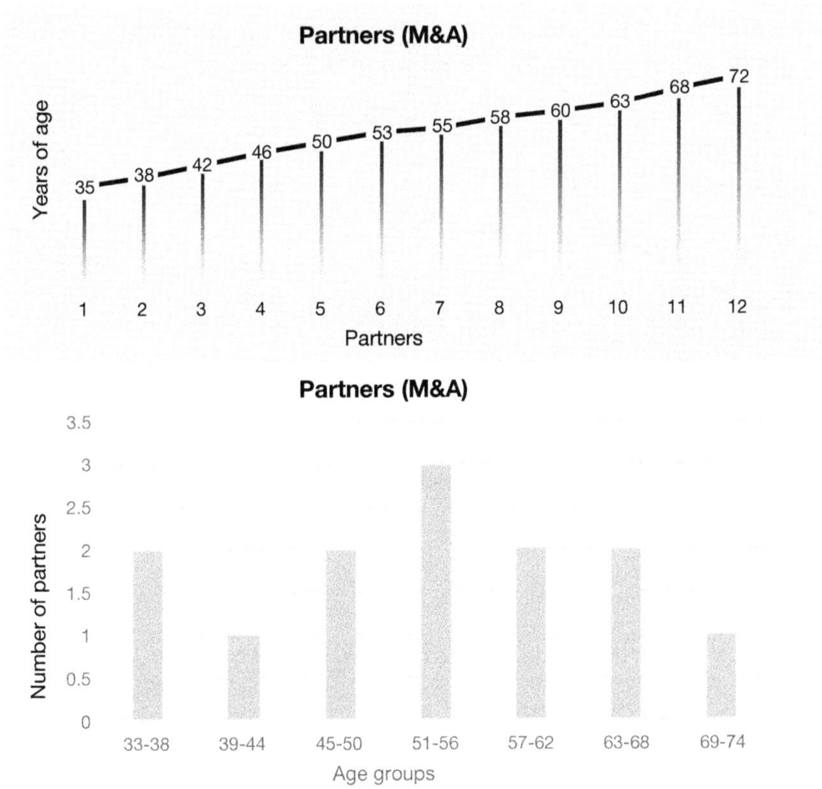

Figure 4: Partner age trendlines.

In Figure 4, we have a (really) smooth trendline with no major gaps. To be direct, they rarely look like this. It isn't abnormal to see gaps of three, four, or five years or more – so, if you see that, you shouldn't be alarmed. But the smoother and more complete the distribution line is, the more comfortable you should be that the firm will continue on making partners at its historic rate.

In Figure 5, you see that this group has been making partners (relatively) recently but does not have a stable of more senior partners. Assuming the group is profitable, it is likely that the firm will be actively pursuing lateral partners and should continue to promote younger partners. A line like this is less than ideal, but does show a recent trend and should be considered a positive. That said, to the degree that you're able, you'll want to determine why, specifically, the group is without more senior representation. Did they lose a group that was never backfilled? If so, why didn't they backfill? What is the firm's plan for the group? Is it possible that the younger group of attorneys is unstable and looking to vacate? It can be less than ideal to see a distribution like this, and to the degree that you are able, you'll want to determine why the group's composition is incomplete.

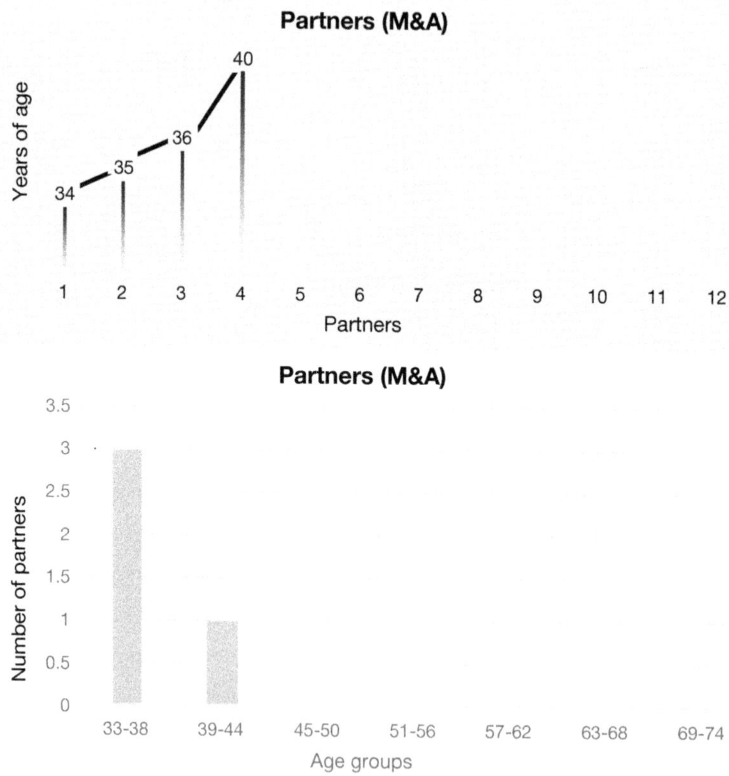

Figure 5: An uneven partner trendline.

In Figure 6, you can see that there is a gap in the middle – a "barbell" of sorts. This, like Figure 5, shows a recent trend of promoting associates to partnership, and it does have a more senior presence, but the gap in the middle should be inspected. Perhaps that mirrors a downturn in the market or a rough patch in the firm's history. Regardless, the recent trend is positive, but you'll want to explore the gap if possible.

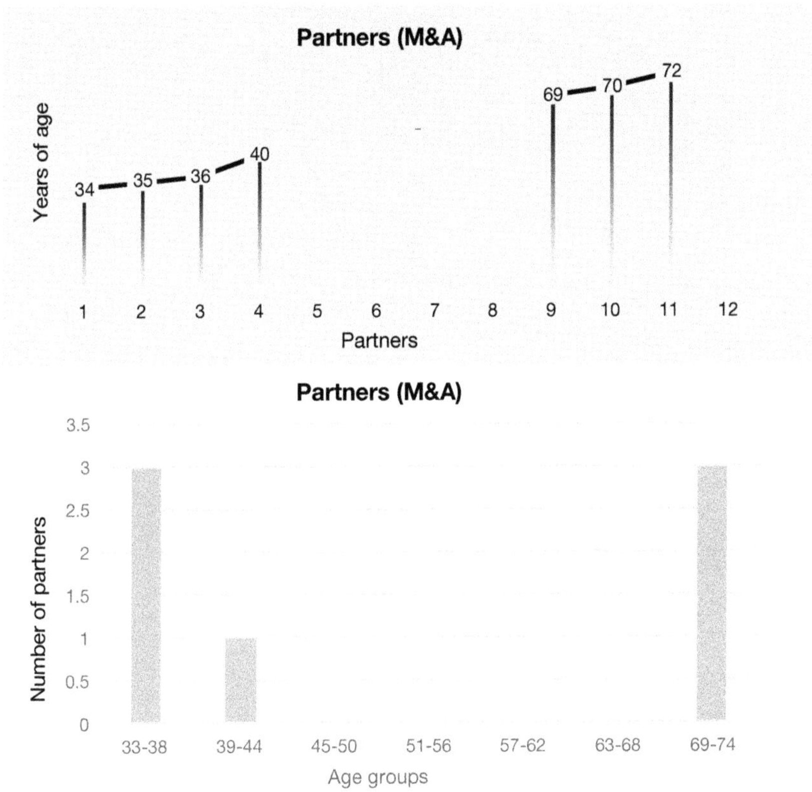

Figure 6: The "barbell" gap.

In Figure 7, there is no recent trend line. It may be tempting to view this from a glass-half-full perspective, but without evidence to logically support the absence, I'll encourage you to view this negatively.

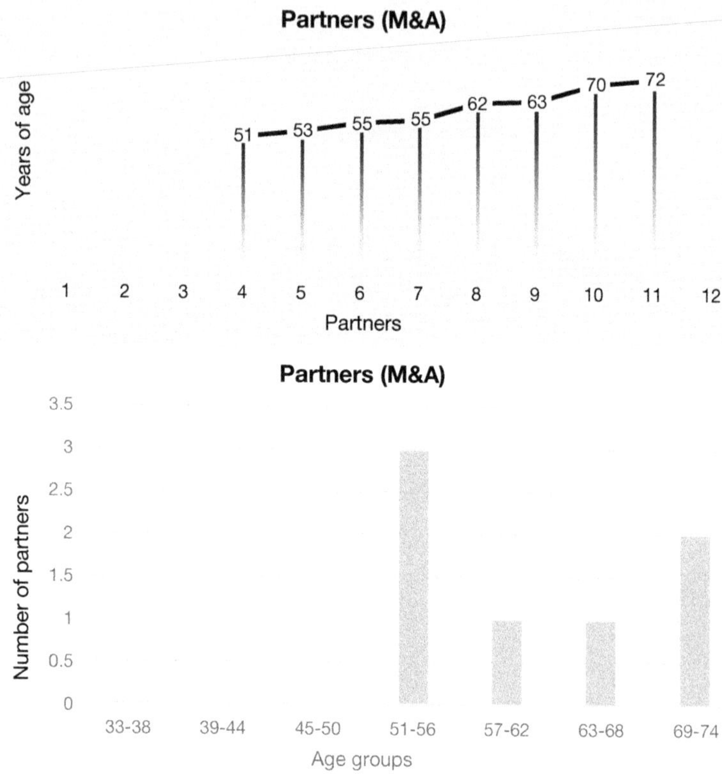

Figure 7: No trend line.

Associate investment

Mentorship

All major firms have mentorship programs; well, at least all firms that I know of. You'd be hard pressed to find a firm that openly admits to not having one. That said, there can be, and often are, major shortcomings where deployment is concerned. By and large, whether or not mentoring actually occurs is a function of the firm's compensation and profitability models. If it is directly and materially incentivized, then the partners are much more likely to do it. Further, if the firm effectively uses leverage for its profitability – i.e., the partners aren't excessively paid based on their own billables – then the partners *may* be keener to mentor. From an observational perspective, you'll want to evaluate mentorship programs at the firm, practice, and individual level.

- *Firm.* How close do the partners seem to get to the associates? Are the associates considered commodities to be consumed or exploited? Or are they human capital to be developed, invested in, and ushered down a path of growth and prosperity? To the degree that you're able, determine what the partnership compensation model looks like. Does it seem to heavily incentivize "management" and "minder" activities? Assuming they have them, what seems to be the general feedback from colleagues on their mentor–mentee relationships?
- *Practice/work.* Here, we're focusing on how helpful and hands-on your assigning and/or deal/matter origination partners are. These don't necessarily have to be your formal mentor, but this can be a good barometer for the positioning of mentor–mentee relationships in the firm-based values hierarchy. That said, if you have questions, how available are the partners? Are they generally happy to engage and help answer them, or do they rush you out the door? Do they explain their thought process when giving answers, or do they simply give you the answer? Even if they are direct (as a result of limited time), are they kind/socially responsive?
- *Individual.* Right off the top, do you (even) have a formal mentor? If so, how much time do they spend with you? Do they seem to be willing, or is it like pulling teeth? Has their advice been personalized and helpful? Do they seem to be sincere in their interactions? Do they seem to (actually) like you? Do you believe that they will champion your cause?

Compensation model

We're not talking here about how much you're being paid by the firm as an associate. Moreso, we're looking at the dynamics of the firm's partner compensation model. Where the previous are observational, to the degree that you're able to acquire compensation model information from the firm you are evaluating, this can provide a more objective view. Consider the following excerpt from *The Failing Law Firm*:[1]

> *"So, does the Team or Confederated nature of the partner class(es) that benefit(s) most from your firm's compensation match up with that of your firm's*

organizational culture? Also, is your firm compensating Management and Minder activities at all? If so, how much? See Figure 8 for an example. If you've determined that your firm's organizational culture is team-oriented like Firm A's, your compensation model should be openly and somewhat aggressively incentivizing activities that are Management and Minder-focused, too. Basically, you are seeing a distribution of capital toward activities that more benefit the collective. Now, take the same organizational culture as above but imagine that your firm's prevailing compensation model is heavily geared toward Finders in particular and little to no compensation is being pushed to Management or Minders. In this case, you may have a problem that requires further examination. If your firm were B, i.e., you are more of a Confederated organizational culture, this wouldn't be a problem as the two criteria are congruent…"

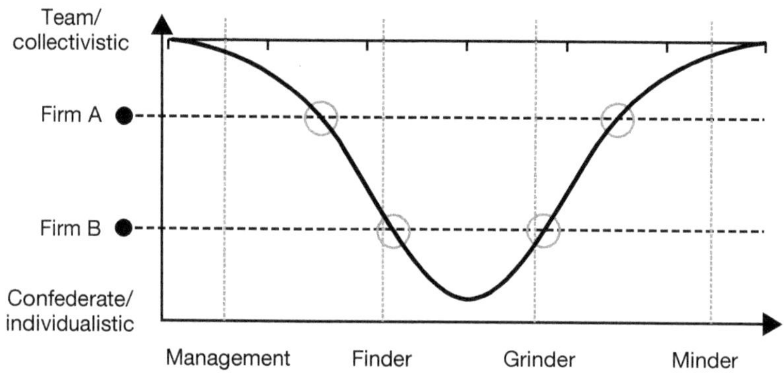

Figure 8: Orientation of the partner classifications.[2]

That paragraph focuses on the congruence between a firm's culture, compensation model, and its allotment of capital and resources. Important to our discussion is where your firm sits on this spectrum. The further it moves toward a team orientation, the more time and resources it will spend on "management" and "minder" activities, which, along with the ever-important responsibility of developing the firm's next generation of lawyers, look something like the following.

Minder:

- Creating and fostering a relationship of trust, credibility, and openness with the client.
- Managing the (sometimes delicate) process of fee collections from clients.

- Managing the progression and execution of ongoing deals/matters, including the delegation of resources, the management of the attorneys working on the deal/matter, and ongoing client relations, among other things.
- Ensuring that the firm's rules, regulations, and P&Ps are adhered to during the course of a deal/matter.
- Determining and assessing the quality standards set forth by both the firm and the client to determine acceptability, and to ensure that they are met.
- Otherwise doing what is necessary to ensure client happiness, retention, and to further develop work.

Management:

- Setting P&Ps and acceptable methods of operation for the firm.
- Creating systems and structures – practice synergy models for example – that help to facilitate the growth and efficiency of the firm.
- Creating and executing hiring and assimilation initiatives to ensure competitive and marketable positions within the first-year and lateral communities.
- Working with compensation committees to establish effective compensation models.
- Actively creating and deploying initiatives that foster the development of a firm's culture.

Your firm will sit somewhere on a spectrum between (a) a purely confederated orientation that subscribes to a purely eat-what-you-kill compensation model, and (b) a purely team orientation that subscribes to a purely lockstep model. As Cravath abandoned full lockstep in 2021, to my knowledge (at the time of writing), Debevoise may be the only other US firm that still uses it. Slaughter and May out of the UK are still holding strong. That said, firms like Slaughter and May, Cravath, Wachtell, and Debevoise either subscribe to, or are functionally much closer to, a lockstep compensation model than firms like Greenberg Traurig or Reed Smith, for instance. This isn't an indictment of the latter firms and/or the eat-what-you-kill system (and its variations) – those firms are highly successful in their own right, and are simply deploying a different tool for a different challenge/environment. That said, in today's legal market the vast majority of firms sit somewhere in between.

So why does this matter? Well, generally speaking, only the most "elite" firms can (or used to be able to) deploy full partner lockstep compensation models (or at least something that closely orbits it), and much of this has to do with the amount of individual effort necessary to develop/maintain business. There's a lot of "stuff" that underpins that statement, and all of it is beyond the scope of this discussion but suffice it to say that on this compensation spectrum, ranging from "team" to "confederated", the closer a firm's model sits to the team orientation (lockstep), generally the more "mentor" friendly it will be.

Leverage

When we look to the essence of a professional services firm's profitability mode, leverage is, or at least should be, the primary concern. However, over the years, as competition has grown and the industry has become more complex, many firms have shifted their compensation models to better incentivize partner billables. When better utilized leverage is more profitable, you may be wondering to yourself, "Why"? Well, that's a good question, but also a (seriously) loaded one, drawing on things like culture, brand quality, marketability, competitive advantage, and more. Suffice it to say, the more heavily a firm leans into the leverage model – i.e., more associates to partners – the more work can, and likely will, be sent down the ladder. This is a good thing, to a point. If a firm's leverage is too high, then the associates might be considered more of a commodity to be consumed. If it is too low, then the partners are doing all of the work, which generally equates to less time spent on the associates.

To be direct, leverage isn't something to be avoided. Usually, the more highly leveraged a firm is, the more profitable it will be, and this is a good thing. Firms like Cleary Gottlieb (5.4:1), Paul Weiss (4.4:1) and Davis Polk (4.3:1) are good examples of this (figures at the time of writing). Exceptions might be very prestigious firms whose business models are to take on highly complex and novel issues. Wachtell is a good example of this. It is incredibly profitable and prestigious, but its leverage is only 2.6:1. The partners are very highly sought after because of their experience with complicated matters, which doesn't lend itself to being "pushed down" to relatively inexperienced associates, so their leverage ratios may be lower, but they are still highly profitable.

At the time of writing, the average leverage in the AmLaw 200 is 1.8 associates for every partner and the standard deviation (St.Dev.) is .9. This is a good benchmark to work with. Your group's leverage should be somewhere between .9 and 2.7. Generally speaking, the closer you get to the mean, the better for our purposes. But, you can (and should) also factor in some higher-level criteria:

- Are you in a practice that lends itself to higher leverage ratios?
- Is your group exceptionally profitable? And if so, is it primarily due to the associates' or the partners' work?
- What do the bill rates look like for the partners? Are they extremely high?
- What kind of write downs and discounts do the partners offer? Are they used often?

With all of that in mind, is the leverage within the group acceptable? You can allow for some latitude on either side based on your answers to the questions above. But, keep in mind that the St.Dev. is only .9, so, moving past that, you are moving closer toward the tails of the bell curve, and that should be viewed with a more scrutinizing lens. You'll want to explore that further.

General hours requirements

A firm's general hours requirement dovetails off its leverage and while it helps you understand how to make your bonus in the firm – important to you, no doubt – it is also a proxy for the underlying values that support and dictate the positioning of associates in the firm's business model. Many firms have an explicit billable requirement (bonus threshold): "Bill this many hours and you'll get a bonus." Oftentimes, associates use this as an indicator of how hard they'll work at the firm. But in reality, there can be a wide spectrum of hours worked in any firm, depending on many factors, such as the type of practice, which partner(s) you're working for, which office you're in, how leveraged your group is, etc. Some firms don't even have an articulated billable requirement because their associates will be billing more than enough to warrant their bonuses; it's not an option. Firms like this will often have you billing 2,200-2,500+ hours. Some firms may have you billing 2,800-3,000 hours, which will leave you very little time to do anything else (of course).

So, what does this have to say about the firm's partnership track? Well, think of it like this. If a firm has you billing 3,000 hours a year, it is unlikely that they commensurately value the development of the other facets of your skill set. Of course, you will develop some of these skills/attributes regardless of the number of hours you bill, but it is unlikely that you'll also be pitching for more business, writing articles, speaking at conferences, building out your network within the firm, etc. So, if you are billing extreme hours like this, to be direct, this firm is likely not as worried about the business development aspects of your skillset and it won't be a criterion for your partnership bid. I'll refer you to our original assumptions/axioms.

Are extreme hours necessarily a bad thing? Should you view far fewer hours as a positive? Well, that depends on your own interests and the firm. Too few hours sent your way could be a barometer for the quality of your work. All things being equal – good economy, firm is busy, work flow is healthy and your peers are busy – low hours generally mean quality and/or personality issues. And while you will have more time to execute other aspects of partnership bid strategy, you'll need to get your own house in order first.

So, what are you looking for? Broadly speaking – and I am speaking anecdotally, here – the 2,200-2,500+ hours region is a good place to be. If you're billing this many hours, there is a signal being sent that your work product is good, you're a sought-after operator, and, depending on how efficient you are with your time, you can engage in other activities in your strategy. It is more challenging, of course, but doable. That said, context can and will play a role in how many hours you should be billing on your own unique partnership track. What are your peers billing? How hard do the partners work? Are you ever turning away work? I leave it to you to parse the individual dynamics of your practice, but making partner isn't easy, and you should expect to be billing close to, if not at, the top of the range of your group (along with executing the other aspects of your strategy). If the top of the range is occupying every waking moment of your time, therefore stripping you of the ability to build up other aspects of your strategy, then you will want to examine the situation further.

With that in mind, how hard are you working? Is it so hard that you'll be challenged in developing and executing the rest of your plan (marketing, networking, sales, etc.)? How hard are your cohorts working? Are they taking on far more hours than you? Assuming they aren't completely buried, this could be a good or bad thing. Perhaps their work product is better than yours, and as such, they are better positioned. They could, however, be less savvy than you and their plan to make partner is simply to work as many hours as possible. I leave it to you to consider the context when making your informed decision.

Summary

So, what do we do with all of this? Is there a scoring methodology? Yes and no. My firm deploys one when working with clients, but weighing the various attributes is a semi-complicated and bespoke task based on context; it is beyond the scope of this chapter. If I was forced to choose one of the above as the most heavily weighted attributes, it would be some function of the strength of your relationship with your mentor(s) and the power/influence that they hold within the firm. No doubt you've heard the saying, "It's who you know". That holds true. At the same time, the (distinct) perception that you will become an autonomously profitable node in the partnership's ranks is going to be paramount. It's hard to overestimate the influence that new and material revenue has on your standing. To accomplish that, you'll need all the help you can get, including, most importantly, the right platform to execute from. Where you – the reader – are concerned, and at the risk of sounding obvious, the more of these criteria your firm has, the better your chances of making partner. A frank assessment can give you a clearer picture of your runway, and help you to better decide how you'll approach it. Good luck!

References

1 *The Failing Law Firm: Symptoms and Remedies*, D. Parnell. American Bar Association, 2015.
2 ©2015 The American Bar Association. Reprinted with permission. All rights reserved. This information or any portion thereof may not be copied or disseminated in any form or by any means or stored in an electronic database or retrieval system without the express written consent of the American Bar Association.

Chapter 3:
Demonstrating readiness for partnership

By Jennifer Bluestein, chief talent and HR officer, Perkins Coie

Introduction

Demonstrating readiness and relevance for partnership is a key requirement for successful partnership; it's not just simply demonstrating a great "run-up" year to partner in terms of productivity. Rather, a successful partner candidate must be able to show long-term commitment to the firm as well as a practice that aligns with the firm's strategy and client base.

This chapter covers the aspects required to show readiness for partnership, as well as what a senior associate can do to prepare for the change and increase in expectations. Senior associates often are frustrated by the long (and increasing) path to partnership, but at the same time, newly promoted partners frequently express they weren't fully prepared for partnership or for the decrease in internal work they received once they had the partner title with the accompanying billing rate.

Being a great lawyer – excellence

First and foremost, the obvious preparation for partnership facet is to become a great lawyer. Malcolm Gladwell wrote an entire book, *Outliers*,[1] on mastery and expertise, famously positing that it takes 10,000 hours to exhibit elite mastery on anything. It is probably no coincidence then that it takes at least six years to become a solid attorney and even longer to be considered someone who can run their own deals and matters.

But what does it mean to be a great lawyer? What does it mean to be able to run deals and matters? There is no agreed-upon definition, but it seems to be a mix of detail-orientation, strong writing and negotiation skills, and, quite importantly, the ability to "see around corners" as many clients say. That ability coincides with experience and judgment, allowing an attorney to see a strategy play out three steps ahead. An attorney who can see around corners is comfortable doing two important things: taking a position that may not immediately make sense and convincing the client that this position is the best way to go. Someone who can play out a matter like a game of chess to either close the deal or win the case (by trial or settlement) is the rare attorney who will have loyal clients.

Another critical element of being a great lawyer is being able to put together and run a team when their practice focuses on large matters. Modern corporations and entities today want attorneys who can efficiently staff and run their matters. They want proper supervision without ten people on every call; they want to know the progression in a matter without having to ask. In essence, they want clear roles and responsibilities on teams without incurring unnecessary expense. More and more, clients are asking for blended fee arrangements, thereby incentivizing the firm to make the highest and best use of each attorney on the matter. An attorney who can use the most qualified and effective associate with the lowest rate is going to win the efficiency and staffing race.

Relatedly, a lawyer who is well-versed in common deal terms for transactional practice will instill confidence in their clients. The same is true for reasonable settlements for litigators. But let's not forget that simply being an outstanding lawyer may not be enough to check the box on attorney capability. One's reputation is also important. Being known as a go-to lawyer, both within your firm and externally, means taking the time to build and maintain that reputation. Whether it's writing articles, speaking at conferences, clerking for well-regarded judges (for litigators), or having worked in government agencies, having a network that holds one in high esteem is a part-time job. The blend of reputation, actual ability, and confidence-inspiring advice with the ability to deliver results will always set an elite attorney apart from the others. And that's a critical factor in demonstrating substantive readiness for partnership.

Have a brand or specialty that sets you apart

Associates often go through a traditional, introductory class at their firms called "Create Your Elevator Pitch" but it's really just a short way of helping attorneys state their unique value in 30 seconds or less. This is a great initial exercise for any attorney to help them understand their special offering. Every attorney worthy of promotion to partner should be able to answer the question, "Why Me?" That is, why would a client hire that attorney over everyone else? Is it that the attorney is the most brilliant IP lawyer who comes up with the most creative arguments to win patents? Is it that the attorney is always there and always responsive? Or is it simply that the attorney has the best track record of winning appeals before the Second Circuit? More likely, there is some combination of factors, such as the attorney is a dual-licensed lawyer between Germany and New York who specializes in crafting trade deals between US and German companies and who happens to be responsive and fun to work with.

In some cases, the attorney has spent the last ten years studying [fill in the blank, but I will use an SEC example here] the SEC and its interpretation of a very specific section of the 1934 Securities Act and has committed their practice to applying those rules to the new banking laws on the horizon. Either way, clients will take a chance on someone who has a reputation for being specialized in just the exact area of need. It gives a comfort level for a client (internal or external) to know their attorney is not simply dabbling in their case.

Self-sustaining network within the firm

As lateral moves have become more and more common, along with remote or hybrid work, it has become increasingly important to get to know more senior attorneys within the firm and communicate one's value and specialized areas of practice to partners in a variety of practice groups and offices. In firms with dozens of offices and thousands of attorneys, it can feel impossible to create a broad internal network of attorneys who understand a senior associate's practice area and want to continually refer that associate new matters. Nevertheless, there are some simple habits that can help a senior associate demonstrate potential to be a successful partner.

Over a period of years, many law firm professionals have seen attorneys try to take some shortcuts to partnership, which we can discuss simply as a cautionary tale. First, the most common shortcut is the senior associate or counsel says, "I need the title of partner in order to be able to develop business". While there may be some perception that the elevated title of partner either creates more of an expectation to bring in business (true) or is a stamp of approval from a firm that encourages a prospective client to trust their work to that attorney (maybe also true), experience tells most law firm leaders that partners who are excellent business generators start out as excellent business generators internally. They instill confidence in the attorneys at their firm and are always busy. Moreover, those individuals tend to have strong networks externally as well, so they are often bringing opportunities to partners at the firm rather than simply waiting for the title of partner.

So what does it mean to create a self-sustaining network within the firm? It means that enough people know what an attorney does to trust them with their clients and matters on a regular basis. For example, one Dallas litigator had a few early successes on a large firm client before being promoted to partner. She became a go-to for all Texas cases that client and the client's lead partner had, which kept her pretty busy for a few years. But shortly after being promoted to partner, she realized that she needed several more people/clients like that. She realized she had spent so much time working on work for that one client and that one client lead partner, she had few other relationships to rely on for a steady flow of work. The new partner changed her approach and reached out to a few key client leads who also had cases in Texas. She asked those client leads to speak with the attorney she had worked for the last several years to act as an internal reference, which they were happy to do. It took nearly a year, but the cases started coming in from different clients and different partners, and her career took off.

Another issue to consider in building the network is the impact of increasing billable rates as people achieve partnership. Once promoted to partner, a senior associate will experience a higher than typical associate-level increase in hourly rate. As a result, partners who may have sent a senior associate work may stop bringing that exact same person into their matters. Some clients will not pay for another partner on a matter, while other partners look at internal reports and feel more pressure to keep associates fully utilized over newly-promoted partners. As a result, it is common for newly promoted partners to express surprise at seeing their hours go down upon promotion. Yet for people in talent and law firm management, this is a common occurrence. Newly promoted partners are generally flat in terms of revenue compared to their last year before promotion. Their hours typically decrease by 15 percent or so, but it's balanced by the increase in their hourly rate. An associate contemplating promotion to partner will insulate themselves to that decrease in hours by ensuring they have a strong network of sponsors who commit to continuing to send them work even after promotion.

Understand the business and where you fit in

An essential success factor for a future partner is two-fold – understanding the business of the firm as well as where one's practice fits into that business and its overall strategy for growth. In today's modern law firm, the clear path is to grow or risk failure. As law firm mergers have increased in terms of frequency and size over the last decade, there seems to be a natural evolution for smaller firms as they struggle to offer clients the level of service and resources clients are demanding. With the exception of 2022, when mid-sized firms experienced more growth than the largest firms, mid-sized firms typically face pressure to scale operations while offering sophisticated support and broad practices to support their clients' needs over a broad platform. While all kinds of platforms can be supportive for a variety of attorneys and practice types, any attorney trying to demonstrate readiness for partner should be able to not only create a business plan, but to tie their business plan to their firm's business plan and overall strategy. While some firms, admittedly, talk about their strategy without having a written strategic plan, or at least not one it shares broadly, many and perhaps most large modern law firms engage in a thoughtful strategic planning process that prioritizes particular practices, sectors, industries, and geographies.

In order to make a successful case for partnership, an attorney should have a basic understanding of what those priorities are and what the firm's rate philosophies might be. For example, a firm may want a diverse array of clients and practices to insulate itself against economic downturns. A firm may want to invest heavily in high-rate M&A work balanced against lower-rate practices that support those M&A deals or stay busy during downturns. A firm that does a lot of tech-focused M&A work may want to also have a tech-focused restructuring and bankruptcy practice to act as a counterweight during a downturn. Similarly, one firm that has a high number of institutional clients that give great volume but at significant discounts may want to also have a high-rate practice in something specialized like White Collar again to balance the high-rate work against the volume, lower-rate work. And finally, a firm may simply want to be a high stakes "bet the company" kind of brand that never reduces rates or takes in small matters. They may not make too many attorneys partner, and they may actually discourage individual business development; they may simply want someone who can do the work at the highest level and be trained to manage client relationships. There are myriad options here, but the point is this – an attorney up for partner should know how the firm positions itself in the market and understand its approach to revenue generation.

For attorneys who don't have a good understanding of the firm's business model or strategy, there are few easy ways to ascertain this information without looking foolish or clueless. The first and easiest step is to seek out a mentor or practice group head, or possibly an office managing partner for firms organized more around offices than practices. Even better, consider asking the same questions of a few people to ensure they are clear on the strategy. If the firm has a strategic plan in writing, make sure you read it and understand it. Ask for a meeting to discuss your preparation for partnership, your business case, and how to better prepare for partnership when the time comes. There are some key questions to ask:

1. What is the firm's strategy for long-term success?
2. Where in that strategy does your practice fall (is your practice one that is needed for long-term success?)
3. If your practice is not critical to the strategy of the firm, where does it fit in to those practices that are essential? Is the firm committed to maintaining and growing your practice?
4. Does your practice face any specific headwinds (loss of clients or talent? Risk of regulatory changes?) that pose challenges for the growth of the practice or sector overall?
5. What does the practice need to ensure or maximize long-term success?
6. What is the expectation for both promoted and lateral partners in terms of origination of work?
7. What does attorney overhead look like and how is it calculated? What percent of associates are profitable? What's the average associate profitability?

Having these discussions early will demonstrate an interest in the business, which in and of itself demonstrates readiness to be an owner. Importantly, the ability to apply the information to one's business plan is further evidence of readiness. Law firm partners want to add partners who are businesspeople who can help expand the pie and maximize the business, lifting all boats; partners do not intentionally add people who feel they deserve to be fed work.

Create a business plan that aligns with the firm's strategy and platform

In some firms, the practice or person sponsoring an associate or counsel for promotion to partner is charged with making the business case, but it is more common for the individual seeking promotion to create their own. A business plan is a detailed strategy with action items that demonstrate an individual has long-term viability to enhance the business of the law firm. It is typically a document that describes the individual's experiences and talents, sources of current work, plans for the future, including future sources of work, and how that fills a gap or need that the firm has now or in the future. For example, a senior associate who specializes in renewable energy with experience in wind energy may be especially attractive if that individual is already managing a firm's day-to-day relationship with a large conglomerate that has recently purchased a company that focuses on wind energy. That individual becomes even more important to the future of the firm if their promotion is blessed by the most senior partner focused on renewable energy who needs that associate in order to grow their book of business. Finally, that individual's promotion becomes even more likely when that senior partner is nearing retirement and says that the individual is part of their succession plan for multiple renewable energy clients.

It can be awkward for someone seeking promotion to state they are the "heir apparent" for a particular book of business, but in any well-managed law firm, succession planning should be part of regular business planning. If it is not, the associate may want to raise the question to their practice group head or office managing partner. Finding out if they are part of the future plan is an important retention issue for anyone on the verge of partnership. While it used to be true that associates within two years of partnership typically stayed put and avoided moving law firms, in the increased mobility of senior associates and partners, this is no longer the case. Law firms that are focused on keeping their clients happy will pay attention to long-term plans for their associates on the verge of partner and for their partners on the verge of retirement, especially at firms that have mandatory retirement age.

An associate's ability to create a business plan demonstrates both a business acumen and a hunger that, if done well, can convince firm leaders this person is part of the future of the firm. Rather than showing a sense of entitlement, a thoughtful business plan can convince other partners that this associate is ready to contribute on a broader scale. While showing a mentor or sponsor a copy of the draft for feedback is helpful, ideally an attorney would create a business plan a year or perhaps two prior to consideration and work with the same sponsor over time to refine it.

Generating a book of business

No chapter on elevation to partnership would be complete (or responsible) without some discussion of the ability to generate revenues. In order to be a viable candidate for promotion, a senior associate should be able to do two things in most firms today – 1) pay for themselves and 2) generate substantial work for others. It goes without saying that law firms rely on a leverage model in which the more senior person generates work for the more junior attorneys; however, there are different ways to analyze how this is done and whether a firm expects a high level of personal production for each partner.

There are different models of partner success, but one element is how future partners might pay for themselves. For example, an attorney who is an outstanding business generator and brings in corporate clients even though they are a litigator might have varied success depending on their firm's expectations for personal productivity. An attorney who can bring in several million dollars in work may not be expected to bill much in terms of hours in personal production. For more junior partners at many firms, the billable expectation may still be 1,800 or higher billable hours. That kind of firm may not even want someone at that level focused on bringing in corporate clients if the billable rate isn't high enough. On the other hand, firms that are more entrepreneurial or who want to invest in the next generation of client development may encourage new partners to focus on business development without an emphasis on billable hours. Related to the idea of creating and getting feedback on a business plan, an associate shows they are ready for promotion when they demonstrate the ability to balance the time and emotional intelligence required to generate billable work with the ability to execute and manage the billable work.

Developing a team, including a lieutenant

The best partners are those who can generate business and are also able to develop a team – training attorneys at all levels, including a right hand or possibly several, which creates the ability to oversee client matters, ensure consistent matter management, and provide the time and freedom for the partner to go meet with more clients and prospects to bring in more work. Unless a firm has unlimited institutionalized work making client generation unnecessary (a rare concept anymore), a partner needs to develop and demonstrate an ability to develop other attorneys at an early stage.

Team management and the ability to develop others is a skill that is fairly difficult to teach in continuing education cases but is a critical skill nonetheless. Attorneys typically develop this skill through a mixture of modeling good partner behavior, excellent planning and organizational skills, and strong communication. An attorney who is ready for partnership is one who can plan out the steps of a matter in advance, assign clear roles and responsibilities to each person involved, follow that plan despite unexpected hurdles, plan for the unexpected, and give ongoing feedback so that those on the team continue to develop their skills. Helpful habits to build a team might include having a kick-off meeting before the work begins to go over all of the above as well as a review at the conclusion of a matter. Partners that fail to build loyal and consistent teams are usually those who are unable to plan ahead and communicate who does what. They are often the kind of supervising attorney who blames others for their own lack of planning or accuses associates of failing to do something but copying others on the team.

The attorney who is ready for partnership is able to plan ahead, give candid feedback (both positive and constructive) without destroying trust or relationships, and give associates of all levels the big picture of what is happening and what is expected on any new matter. The ability to do all of this demonstrates readiness for partnership.

Firm citizenship – what does it mean and why demonstrate it?

An attorney who wants to be considered ready for promotion should be viewed as someone with an eye towards the best interests of the firm and all its people. The best way to do that is to do things that benefit the firm and demonstrate loyalty to the firm and its partners. Respect for the partnership is a critical way to be viewed as a future partner. The senior associates who are best networked within the firm and who are thought of as future owners are those who demonstrate their investment through giving their time to the firm. Associates that serve on associate committees, assist with hiring and mentoring junior associates, support the firm's pro bono and social impact initiatives, and otherwise demonstrate leadership are subconsciously behaving like partners. Accordingly, it becomes an easy stretch for firm leaders to think of them as owners. Just as importantly, those same firm leaders are more likely to know and remember those senior associates as they become eligible for partnership. While these activities take up non-billable time, they create the strong internal networks and profiles that help demonstrate someone is ready for promotion.

There are many ways to demonstrate firm citizenship, and more are being recognized every day. For firms that have summer programs, assisting with on-campus recruiting or attending and planning summer activities is one of the first ways more junior associates can start demonstrating firm citizenship. Committee membership and active participation in those committees is expected as one becomes more senior, and attendance at firm events or firm-sponsored events is part of that expectation as well. As associates become more senior, their involvement in pro bono matters and pro bono committees, along with diversity, equity and inclusion, or social responsibility committees and activities are other good ways to demonstrate citizenship.

A final yet important aspect of preparation for partnership is simply self-education around what partnership entails at any given firm. Every partnership is different, in terms of governance, compensation, and expectations. When an associate is promoted to partner, the expectation is for that associate to become an owner of that business, which involves both upside and risk. Long before elevation to partner, an associate should know the mechanics of the partnership, including whether there is a contribution of equity, also known as a buy-in for partnership, and other terms in the partnership agreement.

Regardless of which kind of law firm is at issue, an attorney who is demonstrating readiness for partnership is able to ask thoughtful questions and demonstrate an understanding of what life as a partner is actually like. Associates tend to assume that life gets easier once they have the title of partner when, in actuality, the expectations and pressure increase. By having a true understanding of all the factors that lead to true readiness for partnership, an attorney is more likely to demonstrate those core capabilities that lead to long-term success as a partner.

References

1 Gladwell, M, *Outliers: The Story of Success*. Little, Brown and Company; San Francisco, CA. 2008.

Chapter 4: Making the choice about partnership

By Claire Rason, director, Client Talk

Whether or not associates progress to partnership comes down to choices. There is a choice to be made by the firm doing the promoting. However, what is often forgotten is that there is also a choice to be made by the individuals themselves. More often than not, finding answers to the questions "Do I want to make partner?" and "Can I be a partner?" is something that professionals struggle with.

In this chapter, we explore some of the reasons why women in particular might choose not to progress. We think about the impact that this has on gender parity at partnership level and suggest how this can be addressed. What is behind our individual choices and how can we reframe the questions "Do I want to?" and "Can I?" to help women succeed?

Why we must remember it's a choice

When we start our careers, we nervously sit down in our first interview, well-prepared and eager to impress. It is easy to forget, in that moment, that interviews are an opportunity to find out more about our potential future employer. Even with the inevitable "Are there any questions for us?" closing query, the fresh-faced interviewee is much more likely to reel out some pre-prepared questions to demonstrate they have done their research, rather than ask anything too hard-hitting.

Interviews, though, are as much about you testing your potential employers as they are for them to test you. The more senior you get, the more this comes to the fore. You start to hold more of the cards and your interviewer has to start to demonstrate why they want you. Potential employees have power; particularly when the employment market is buoyant. There is an enhanced understanding on both sides of what it takes for the relationship to work. Both sides need to commit.

On the road to partnership, choice is also present. However, becoming a partner is seldom something that happens as a result of a one-and-done interview. It is more commonly a journey that professionals find themselves on, one which unfolds over time. The question "Is this for me?" is something that will be turned over in the professional's mind, both consciously and unconsciously, at different points on that journey.

Whilst the promoting firm needs to back the associate, the reason that professionals don't progress often falls to individual personal choice. In other words, many associates turn their backs on partnership. Some do not put themselves forward, whilst others actively make it known that it is not for them.

Personal choice is often overlooked by the firm's recruitment panels and committees. The decision-makers in a firm typically act on the belief that if an associate is good enough, they will want to become partner. This belief, whether explicitly stated or not, comes to the surface in initiatives designed to get people into the existing model of partnership, not stopping to explore whether they want to get there. It also comes through in the conversations that happen with associates who are earmarked for partnership. It is taken as read that these people will want to pursue it. There is no space for fears, doubts, or concerns.

Given the perceived holy grail of partnership, professionals who doubt whether it is for them are in a difficult position. The decision-making that goes on inside an associate's mind is kept secret. They are not asked whether they want to progress, and what doubts they might have. To voice any concerns, unprompted, would be to question the prevailing viewpoint. Associates fear that expressing concerns might show a lack of commitment, which could hinder that individual's chances should they decide to go for it. Safer then to keep one's views to oneself until the choice has been made.

Sadly, once the decision is made, and is played back into the firm, it is too late to unpick. Now, some might question whether it is right or wrong to question individual choices. However, if these choices result in gender imbalance at partnership level, which I believe they do, it perhaps makes sense to pause on this issue of choice. In pausing, we notice a need for the decision-making process to be explored in the open.

In this chapter, we will discover how openly thinking about choices will benefit women. The benefits don't stop there; this will also benefit men and diversity initiatives at large.

If you are reading this book as an associate, thinking about, and discussing, whether you want to be a partner, I would invite you to put the book down now and to jot down what doubts, fears, or questions you might have. What do you think when asked the question, "Do you want to make partner?" We will invite you to explore these thoughts again later in this chapter.

Gender imparity at partnership

Before we explore the link between choice and gender, let's think about the prevailing landscape. In my own study of diversity, The Class of 2002: Women in Law,[1] I aimed to find out whether, if I had stayed in law, I would have made partner. I started as a trainee with a leading global law firm and my research traced the journeys of my fellow trainees (the so-called "Class of 2002").

The Class of 2002 started out as 57 percent women. A total of 73 percent of the Class of 2002 stayed in law, leaving a population with a roughly equal gender split. However, of the total Class of 2002, only 23 percent of women hit the highest level in law, whilst 59 percent of the men have achieved that status. Whichever way the data was cut, men outperformed women. It wasn't that women had left private practice, or fee earning; some did, but so did some men.

Outwardly, there was no reason why the intake could not have achieved gender parity at partnership level.

The study debunked many myths: that it is about role models; that it is because women leave to have children; or that it is about access to the right work. It did find evidence that suggested that the 24/7 culture, prevalent in many law firms, played a part. However, the impact of culture, often described as "How we do things around here", was compounded when seen from the perspective of "Who does things around here". The study uncovered key differences in how respondents described themselves and how they described partners. Partners tended to be associated with male-gendered traits. Interestingly, both men and women, partners and non-partners, had a similar view of the traits prevalent in partners.

The key traits that appeared in a description of partner, but which were lacking in how respondents described themselves were *ambitious*, *assertive*, and *strong*. These are traits that are male-gendered, stereotypical male traits being agentic. The traits that were used to describe partners discounted stereotypically feminine traits, women stereotypically being designated as communal.

Much has been written about the impact of bias and stereotype and how these play out in systems. A particularly relevant piece of research is that which set forward the theory of gendered organizations, espoused by Joan Acker.[2] The reason this theory is of interest here is that she put forward the view that organizational structures can be gendered (when hitherto they were assumed to be gender-neutral) and also, she examined the who. Acker described the ideal worker within these organizations as someone who "*is a rational, strong leader, committed to work and unencumbered by family*". In these organizations, mothers are judged as less competent, a finding that also played out in the Class of 2002. Women found it harder to show they were good enough to be partner upon having children, in a way that wasn't a problem for men.

Others[3] have described what narratives are heard within these firms that reinforces the notion of a gendered organization. These narratives include:

- Employees reporting that long hours and visibility yield status and rewards.
- Employees demonstrating dedication through long hours.
- Employees describing networking as key.

All of these narratives are prevalent in law firms.

More recent writings, including the Class of 2002, have started to question how this notion of the ideal worker affects not only the prospects of females, but also harms men. Women don't progress, but men also have to measure themselves against the ideal worker, which comes with its own problems. Legal professionals are increasingly at risk of burnout, and, in one recent study,[4] 69 percent said they had experienced mental ill health.

The impact of choice

How do these findings link with choice? The Class of 2002 study found some evidence to suggest women are prevented from reaching the top; however, it also found lots to challenge the assumption that they wanted to get there. Non-partners showed higher life satisfaction than partners (across both genders).

The "always on" culture was seen to negatively affect both men and women. However, the study found that women feel able to say no to partnership in a way men are not. This is bound up in expectations, prescriptive and descriptive stereotypes, confidence, and limiting beliefs.

When coaching female leaders, coaches often hear that they want to step back from their positions. They feel they no longer have boundaries between home and work. The 24/7 culture of the professional services firms they are in is too much. They are prepared to turn down, or give up, partnership to solve that problem.

Male "coachees" have different reflections. Whilst they too might want a work–life balance, or don't like the culture, or don't feel "part of the club", unlike the women, they feel that if they choose not to become partner it is going against what is expected. One male interviewee in the Class of 2002 report felt that they had been brave to turn down partnership and that others had questioned their choice at the time. Another, who stepped away from partnership at a senior level, struggled with the fact he was no longer fulfilling *"the male stereotype of being the main breadwinner"*.

The result of the choices that are made is that partnerships contain a cohort of men – and women – who have chosen to be there, but crucially they also contain a cohort of men who may have wanted to leave but who felt unable to do so. Stereotypes mean they are unable to truly challenge the status quo. Partnership also excludes those women who chose a different path. They are equally unable to challenge the status quo – they don't have the badge of partner. Their choices result in gender imparity. Individual cases are lamented, but the system isn't changed.

Is it about when we have to make a choice?

Choice is personal, but there are commonalities that influence choice along gender lines. The Kaleidoscope Career Model (KCM)[5] describes how three parameters (authenticity, balance, and challenge) influence the way we view our careers and suggests these things shift over the course of an individual's lifespan. The model suggests these parameters guide us in our careers with certain things taking precedence at different times.

What is interesting is that women become interested in balance mid-career. This is not just about family but about *"non-work issues"* that *"encompass a woman's own physical and psychological wellbeing, her friends – especially if she is single or has no children – volunteer activities, hobbies, and spirituality"*. Men take a different journey and balance is less important for them mid-career, coming more into focus later on.

Mid-career (30s/40s) is often when men and women are thinking about whether partnership is for them. The KCM therefore provides another layer of insight into why men and women might choose different things at different times. Where there is a perception that partnership will mean less balance, this will be a key factor for women, in a way that it might not be for men. We refer again to the aforementioned narratives found in gendered organizations.

For women, as balance comes into focus before they have made partner, the impact is that they might choose not to become partner. The notion of balance does not fit the construct of an ideal worker. Ironically though, this choice might actually make it harder for them to achieve balance in the long-run.

The partners we speak to often say that they have been better able to balance their interests after being made up. They have more freedom to set their own agenda. They no longer feel as judged. Men become more interested in balance later on in their careers, often when they are already partners. We hear from many male partners that they are able to do school drop-offs etc. because of their roles as partners. These views do not get widely shared at a firm level, and often these partners are more senior, rather than newly appointed, so these perspectives are not considered when decisions are made at senior associate level.

The KCM provides another example of how our individual choices are influenced by parameters that we do not necessarily examine openly. As with all models, everyone is an individual, and there will be differences. However, if nobody discusses how we make choices, and how they might play out, it is easy to see how the decision-making process can be flawed. Alternative perspectives aren't shared. One might also ask, can the choice be a real choice if it is made in secret, and, in part, influenced by unconscious thoughts and unseen external influences?

Firms at this juncture often say that they do question choices; however, we often hear that individuals are questioned about "What can we do to get women into partnership?" rather than be asked "What was behind your individual choice?". These are two very different questions and elicit very different answers.

The confidence factor

Another important factor when it comes to choice is confidence. This is key to answer the question that many associates will have considered: "Am I cut out to make partner?". Associates are unlikely to express that they think they are not capable of being a partner. If they are not confident that they have what it takes to be partner, perhaps struggling with imposter syndrome, why would they share that?

Whilst some professionals might choose not to progress, that doesn't mean they are choosing to leave the firm. Some do, but a large proportion will stay at the firm in a different role. Surely, it would be career suicide to say out loud that you are not competent.

What is confidence? It is faith in our skills and capabilities. It is being sure of ourselves. Studies have shown that confidence can have an impact on the representation of women in senior leadership roles. In particular, a recent study found that female self-confidence is impacted by assumed masculine characteristics in leadership. This makes sense – why should women be confident in assuming characteristics that haven't served them to get to where they are?

Given that the role of partner is associated with masculine-gendered traits, there is a risk that this will impact female confidence. Female lawyers are more likely than their male counterparts to lack faith in their abilities to adopt the dominant style of leadership in their firm. They are unsure whether they will be able to 'manage like a man'. This can be compounded by programs that teach them to lead like the stereotypical partner, rather than focusing on leveraging individual talents.

The finding that self-confidence is a factor aligns with the Grey et al.[6] study, which showed that that coaching is a way to create change in gendered organizations. I have also seen the power of coaching first-hand and use it as a way to reframe what it means to lead and what it means to be a partner.

Gray et al. set out to find what impact a leadership development program could have on female leaders' self-confidence, self-esteem, and career development. They found that:

> *"Coaching, both individual and group, can have a powerful effect on promoting reflection, self-confidence and focus. The group coaching in particular, helped to generate a feeling that many of the experiences and problems of women leaders were collectively shared. This was important because many of these women leaders faced the challenges of achieving a work-life balance, having to demonstrate an impact in their work and also having responsibilities for both children and often-elderly parents. Group coaching specifically helped in the generation of positive group dynamics which meant that some groups decided to continue after the end of the program – becoming developmental networks."*

The result of this played out in more women advancing in the organization at the heart of the study. What this shows us is that thoughts such as "I am not good enough at X" or "I cannot do Y" need to be brought to the surface, challenged, and explored. Coaching is a way of digging down and doing just that.

Common concerns

In the remainder of this chapter, I look at some of the common concerns that females in particular express and examine how these can be rethought and reframed. The common reasons that we hear from female lawyers as to why they chose not to progress their careers beyond associate level include:

- "I am no good at business development/I can't shake the tin."
- "I don't think I can lead in the way I see other partners leading."
- "I couldn't be a partner and juggle my other commitments."
- "It doesn't look like any fun."

Where do these thoughts come from? What are they trying to cover? Part of this thinking will be done at a conscious level; however, an even larger part will happen unconsciously. It will be influenced by the narratives the associates hear. It will be influenced by stereotypes. It will also cover deeper insecurities, including imposter syndrome and fear of failure.

Limiting beliefs are ideas that we hold about ourselves that prevent us from performing at our best. They come up frequently in coaching conversations. Coaches explore the truth of these statements; they encourage clients to look at the resources they have to overcome them. They think about how to reframe the belief to bring about change. Here I am going to explore some of the common reasons that are surfaced.

The fear of business development

> *"One of the reasons I didn't make partner was because I am no good at business development."*

This is a statement that I have heard from several female lawyers as the reason why they decided not to progress to partnership. I know these women. I know that they are well-respected. They had sponsors wanting them to succeed in their firms. The firms were dumbfounded when they heard that they did not want to progress. They had (and still have) no idea this was the reason.

The belief that to be a partner means being good at winning work is espoused over and over. Even in this book, you will read about how to "do" business development. It is important. However, misunderstanding what business development is can get in the way of women progressing. It is also a concrete example of how confidence can hold women back, and how open and honest dialogue can be a solution.

It is often the case that, for professionals on the path to partnership, advice is given to help them "up their BD game". This is understandable – associates have to put forward a business case to be made up and invariably that needs to show strong relationships and the ability to bring in business. They need a plan and numbers.

Many firms don't provide the skills to do this until it is too late and by the time associates need to "up their BD game" they are fearful, lack confidence, and it becomes a barrier. For women, it becomes a reason to step away from partnership; for men, it can become a barrier to doing business development. For the latter, better not to admit that they are no good; once they make it they can win work and avoid the bits they do not enjoy. For females, it is yet another reason to believe that they do not fit.

I believe that business development is important, and that business development skills need to be introduced early on. However, as with leadership skills, they need to be deployed authentically. Business development needs to be understood in terms of its purpose. The purpose of it is to create, nurture, and maintain relationships. For that, professionals need to develop enhanced self-awareness. Why? Simply, there is no one right way of achieving the purpose of business development. With increased self-awareness, associates can deploy their strengths to nurture relationships. It is not about morphing into an alpha rainmaker. For some, this will be their authentic style and clients will respond to that. For others, this will be inauthentic and therefore unlikely to work. The beauty of it is that, if a firm contains a combination of approaches, it is much more likely to appeal to a broader range of individuals.

Unless you are a sole practitioner, or in a small firm, you are likely to be in a place where you have a range of professionals who are all good at different things. You will also have a team of marketing and business development experts who are good at business development – that's what they do! Business development is about relationships; in large firms, complex webs of relationships. These are created, maintained, and nurtured by teams working together. Understanding what you bring to the team is key. Understanding who can fill the gaps that you can't, and being open to being vulnerable – admitting that someone else is better placed to do something – is arguably the best way to "do" business development. This myth that one person has to be good at everything is damaging and unnecessary.

Many of the skills that result in good business development are skills that women have in spades. Being able to lead a team, or being able to develop individuals, or being able to offer commercial and innovative solutions to clients. All these things make the firm attractive to clients (and employees). These all benefit client relationships and will result in work being won. But, because business development is so often equated with shaking a tin and negotiating fees, these qualities get lost and devalued. They are rarely included as part of an individual's business case for partnership.

Authentic leadership

The majority of men and women surveyed described partners in male-gendered terms. This was true of the Class of 2002, but I have re-run the questionnaire with different groups outside of it, and they have yielded the same results. It is not uncommon, when I coach women, to hear that they are struggling to adapt to a style of leadership that does not come naturally to them. Females ask, "How can I be like X person?". In these firms, there tends to be a universally perceived way of being a partner.

One of the reasons why diversity is seen as producing greater results is because it provides for enhanced perspectives, ideas, and creativity. This is important to remember. We should not be looking to create a partnership army of clones. To be a good partner you should be able to lead in a way that is authentic for you.

As with business development, the starting point should be to understand what the end result is that you are looking to achieve. There are multiple things that partners need to achieve; from leading a team, to delivering for clients, and growing the firm. The question associates should ask is not, "How can I be like X?", but rather, "How can I achieve what is needed in a way that is authentic to me?".

A lot is written about authentic leadership. The starting point, again, is self-awareness. Authentic leadership is often described in terms of qualities. They are said to lead with heart rather than ego, they are good at cultivating relationships, and they lead with values and principles.

Associates reading this: think about what your values are. What skills do you have and how can you leverage those skills to achieve results? Your values and skills might be similar to what partners in your firm are already doing, or they might be fundamentally different. If they are different, can these co-exist? That last question is one that you might want to explore with members of your firm.

If you have a role in a firm and you are thinking about how to develop authentic leadership skills in your associates (or maybe even your partners), I would invite you to shift from focusing on how individuals need to be when they are a partner, to exploring what skills associates already have that can be leveraged to achieve results. This moves the conversation from "You need to be like this" to "Who are you and how can you leverage that to achieve results as a partner?". This increases self-awareness, authenticity, and confidence.

Juggling other commitments

We have already seen that many partners express the view that balance is achievable when you make partner. There is also a chapter in this book that focuses on wellbeing and the challenges and opportunities of partnership.

Many of the concerns that women raise around balance are rooted in the construct of an ideal worker. Females tell us that whilst they see other females in partnership, many of those fit this notion of an ideal worker, having perhaps forgone having children, or being in a situation where their life partners or nannies do the majority of the childcare. They feel that this is not something open to them. This is an issue that is often discussed privately outside of law firms but continues to be seen as taboo within them.

This is a big challenge and one that hits at the heart of some of the systemic barriers that prevent firms from achieving gender parity. Transformational change is hard. However, we all have the ability to start to change the landscape and the way that we start to do that is through our narratives. As we have seen, narratives can reinforce stereotypes and biases. They can also highlight change and challenge those things.

There is an increasing recognition in firms that the role of partner can be delivered in many different ways. The pandemic has created a shift in the way we deliver and where we deliver. Technology will increasingly change the way that partners add value to their clients in the future. These stories need to be shared. Narratives are there to be challenged and questioned.

If you are struggling to see how you can have balance, I would invite you to consider the following questions.

- Is it true that you cannot be a partner and have balance?
- What evidence can you find to prove this wrong?
- Who can you explore this with?
- If you had a magic wand, how would you solve this?

If you are an associate – male or female – and your choice of whether or not to progress is being affected by a perceived lack of balance, test it. You might find that with all the facts on the table you make a different decision.

"It didn't look like fun"

Being someone you are not, and trying to fit into a model that does not align with your values, is not fun. However, we are often caught in traps of our own making. You have a choice as to whether to progress. Make sure that your decisions happen in the open. If you decide partnership is not for you, that is okay, just don't bury the conversation. You might well find that others are feeling the same way.

I want you now to refer back to the questions and concerns that you wrote down at the beginning of the chapter. Use these following questions to explore them:

- Is it true? What evidence can you find to prove this wrong?
- Where might this belief or concern have come from?
- Who can you explore your decision with?
- If you had a magic wand, how would you solve this?

Getting to gender parity

Many existing programs, whilst well-meaning, fail to deliver the intended results. They fail to address the issue of choice; it is assumed that these women want to make partner, but they need support to look like existing partners. This prevents honest conversations taking place. In addition, many female leadership programs are viewed by the participants as being a way to "fix" them rather than to challenge the prevailing model. This can make women resentful, and it can further bury the conversation around choice.

Choices and challenges need to be more openly discussed by both genders. Each gender has different challenges, and coaching (particularly individual combined with group coaching) has been shown to help females increase their self-confidence and succeed where they might not otherwise have. Coaching isn't about imposing, it is about empowering. It is about helping females see that they have what it takes to challenge the status quo and be authentic. These individual women will in turn become agents for change and help to move towards a more transformational change in the industry.

However, authentic leadership should be for everyone. Allowing individuals to be individuals will generate an environment in which difference is embraced and different styles of partner can co-exist and work together. Those law firms that achieve this will create a partnership that is more than the sum of its parts.

Implications for diversity initiatives more broadly

I believe that achieving gender parity is the right thing to target. The leadership of a firm should be reflective of those it leads, as well as society at large. Not only that, but diversity brings with it so many benefits that firms are missing out on. This is largely recognized and many firms have declared that they need to do better and are working to do so. Partnership not only needs to be representative in terms of gender, but also other diverse metrics (demographic and cognitive). Diversity is about people. The answers to many of our challenges lie with our people and truly understanding them.

Whilst this chapter has focused on gender, it has broader implications for diversity initiatives more generally. It is challenging to think that our choices are not individual. However, the statistics continue to suggest that they might not be as individual as they seem. As law firms grapple with how to be more equitable, the issue of choice should be brought to the surface. Law firms need to create environments that people want, and are able, to say yes to, at all levels.

It is not for anyone to impose choice on another, but I would argue that choices should be questioned when they result in talent choosing to step away, or to pause their careers. We should be curious as to what is behind individual choices. We should explore what needs to be done to make them choose otherwise. There is rich learning to be had and, rather than striving to ensure that everyone fits the existing model, we should challenge ourselves to think about how the existing model needs to change in order that everyone can thrive.

References

1 www.clienttalk.co.uk/reports

2 Acker, J. (1990). Hierarchies, Jobs, Bodies: A Theory of Gendered Organizations. *Gender & Society*, 4(2), 139-158.

3 Gray, D., De Haan, E. and Bonneywell, S. (2019), "Coaching the 'ideal worker': female leaders and the gendered self in a global corporation", *European Journal of Training and Development*, Vol. 43 No. 7/8, pp. 661-681. www.emerald.com/insight/search?q=Erik%20De%20Haan

4 www.lawcare.org.uk/life-in-the-law/

5 Sullivan, S. E., and Mainiero, L. (2008). Using the Kaleidoscope Career Model to Understand the Changing Patterns of Women's Careers: Designing HRD Programs That Attract and Retain Women. *Advances in Developing Human Resources*, 10(1), 32–49.

6 See note 3.

Chapter 5:
The business and personal traits of a partner

By Pippa Blakemore, The PEP Partnership LLP

A partner in a law firm has an extraordinarily complex and demanding role. A partner is expected to be the embodiment of an entire commercial business, encapsulating almost all the departments in one person.

A partner must be a strategist, leader, manager, team-builder, work-winner, work doer, financial controller, debt-collector, and compliance officer. A partner's skills need to range from the visionary, through practical management, while at the same time focusing on the micro-detail of obscure areas of law.

This chapter analyses three key categories of skills – strategic, leadership, and management – and features the personal characteristics required to fulfil this multiplicity of responsibilities.

Strategically, partners are required to evaluate objectively where the firm, its services, offices, departments, sectors, and practice areas are now, where they want to be, and how to get there. Leadership requires partners to be loyal, committed to the strategy and facilitating its implementation, constructively managing risk and overcoming problems and challenges on the way.

Managerially, while trying to achieve the firm's vision and implement its mission, a partner will also be expected to run the business daily – clients, cases, matters, the firm, offices (local, national, and international), sectors, departments, practice areas, a range of permanent or temporary teams and individuals.

Personally, to achieve those expectations, a partner must have many individual qualities, which are fundamentally based on self-discipline, self-awareness, and self-control. This chapter identifies the core traits required to be a partner, gives examples of when to use them, tips on how to make the most of them, the benefits, and why they are important.

The aim is to make this chapter a personal action plan and checklist, so approach it with a highlighter and pen – physical or electronic – and keep this as a working document.

Strategic

Every partner needs to know, thoroughly support, and promote the firm's vision, mission, culture, and values, internally and externally. The more senior the partner becomes, the more they will be involved in the creation, development, monitoring, and measurement of the progress of the strategic plan at firm, office, and department level.

The strategic plan needs to be reviewed regularly and reliably, at pre-agreed times. If the plan is not achieving its goals and targets, it needs to be modified or remedial action taken, promptly, where and when necessary.

The vision should incorporate where the firm is going in the short-, medium- and long-term. The vision statement should be short, memorable, and repeatable, so that everyone in the firm relates to it and is proud of it.

The mission is how the firm is going to get there and includes who the firm will work for, geographic locations, the services it delivers, the work it will do, and the corresponding supporting organizational structures. Factors to consider are the target client profile, annual income targets for the firm by office, department, sector, and practice area, profile of the firm to be promoted, size of firm desired, turnover, and profitability. Culture and values are the foundations on which the firm provides services to and advises its clients.

The partner needs to know this for their office, department, sector, and practice area and teams. The strategic plan needs to be communicated throughout the firm so that everybody knows where the firm is going and each individual's contribution to its success.

The partner must know and understand all these strategic objectives for every single one of their clients and on every matter, and ensure that everyone working on the matter knows and understands these.

A good way of checking is to ask members of the department and the matter team, in the corridor, or at the start of a meeting, what the strategic objectives, vision, and mission are for the client. This helps to focus, prioritize on behalf of the client, and make judgments on what is important to the client or the matter.

Leadership

A partner must distinguish the range of leadership techniques available and have the flexibility to use them appropriately. Previously, a leader could have their own style and be tagged as a certain type of leader. Modern leadership requires the leader to adapt their techniques to the situation or the individual.

There are many theories of leadership, but the four techniques most relevant for partners in law firms to choose from and to use appropriately at different times according to need are as shown in Table 1.

Table 1: Four relevant leadership techniques.

Technique	Features	Benefits and uses	Risks
Inspire	Partner inspires with: • Vision of firm • Vision of office/department/ practice area • Big body language • Future and long-term aspirations • Great concepts • Intangible ideas • Everything with passion and authority and conviction	Inspires clients and internal teams and gives confidence: • Annual conferences • Away days • Partners' conferences • Departmental reviews • Managing change • Motivational • Gives hope • Re-motivation after a crisis	• No credibility unless followed by action • Analysis by recipients or audience might find little substance and therefore such a technique might generate the opposite reaction than that desired • If used in the wrong circumstances it can be damaging
Dictate	Partner tells people what to do: • No questions allowed • No objections permitted • No questions asked by partner • No checking of people's reaction or feelings • No checking by partner of understanding	• In a crisis • When the partner does know best • Short, rigid deadlines • In an emergency, e.g. fire	• It is increasingly less acceptable as a leadership technique • Must be obvious why it is necessary • May result in outcome partner did not want, because no checking of understanding or monitoring of impact
Consult	Partner makes final decision, but: • Explains context • Sets objectives • Asks questions • Listens to the answers • Responds and adapts • Acknowledgement and credit given to input from others involved • Makes people feel that their opinion counts	Building a strong team and team spirit: • Generating respect • Developing mutual understanding and knowledge • Developing individuals • Enables partner to understand how people approach problems and discussions	• Needs time • Must be genuine • Must be seen as sincere consultation, not just superficial • Need to give feedback so that the team can learn

continued on next page

Technique	Features	Benefits and uses	Risks
Collaborate	Partner and the team make the decision together. Partner: • Sets context • Generates group discussion to agree and understand objectives, priorities, and outcomes. • Works with team • May delegate to individual or team to make own decisions and then gives input	• When a decision needs to be supported and implemented by all • When ownership of decision is required from individual or team • Team development and individual development • Enables partner to identify how people think	• Respect all input, however weird it might seem • Record all suggestions, so even if one suggestion is not used, the person who made it sees that it has been recorded • No negatives • No criticism of ideas • No belittling of thoughts • Monitoring and measuring outputs and outcomes • Feedback and lessons learned

As a partner, you need to adapt techniques to the requirements of the situation or context. However, there are some consistent fundamental requirements to be an outstanding strategist and leader as a partner.

As a leader you must passionately and vocally believe in and support the vision of the partnership for you to ensure its implementation. A strong firm needs unity among partners, and it is your responsibility to be part of that unified front. It is very unsettling for junior members of the firm if they perceive disunity at the top that permeates down.

A leader must be able to put their head into the other person's head and facilitate the same approach from your teams. For example, if you are dealing with a client's contract, don't deal with it in terms of you as them, but rather think about them as them. For you, it may be just a contract. For your client, it could determine the success or failure of their life's work.

This applies to delegating work. If you say to a junior attorney, "It will only take you an hour" (because that is what it would take you – i.e., you in their position) and the junior takes four hours, they may be afraid to tell you and may not time-record their actual time taken.

The unintended consequences of a partner dictating to somebody how long a piece of work will take, with no reassurance of "Come back to me if it is taking longer" may be huge. If this is repeated, it accumulates into regular underquoting of the time taken and hence cost. If the next fixed-fee estimate for the same or similar work is based on previous figures, the matter will be massively underquoted, which could lead to financial loss for the firm and department.

As a leader, you must lead by example. This applies to everything you as a partner are responsible for. It undermines your credibility to say one thing and do another.

You must be open to learning from everything. Even if something goes badly, ask yourself, "What can I learn from this? What can the team learn from this? What can individuals learn from this? How do we apply this learning in future?" It helps to take the sting out of an awful situation and turn it into a useful experience.

Have a "no blame, no shame" de-brief on all matters and situations. For those that went well, analyze why, and how the good lessons from this can be applied in future.

For those that went badly, then do it in the following order, with a free-for-all brainstorm:

- "What went well?" This starts the de-brief on a positive note.
- "What would we do differently next time?" This approach is important. Note it is not phrased as "What went badly?" The reason is that the latter question will engender fear, defensiveness, and self-protection.

Asking how we might do things differently is likely to lead to positive and constructive suggestions, such as "I could have drafted that more effectively." "I should have started earlier." The lessons are not imposed by the leader but generated from open suggestions from the individuals themselves, which makes them more likely to remember them, have ownership of their responsibility, and apply any lessons in future.

Management and business

Try the following quiz. Mark yourself out of ten in the right-hand column.

Management and business skills of a partner **Check that you do the following with your clients and your teams.** I ...	**Mark 1-10** **1 = lowest** **10 = highest**
1. Ask "open" questions to get all the information before giving advice or instructions (What, Who, When, Where, Why, How, How much).	
2. Ask "closed" questions that give a "Yes" or "No" answer, to confirm my understanding of any situation or person (sentences starting with Is, Can, Do, Have, Are).	
3. Listen – with my ears and eyes. Match body language to words.	
4. Chair and participate in productive meetings with agenda and time awareness.	
5. Build strong, united, integrated, supportive, motivated teams.	
6. Give appraisals/reviews that contribute to achievement of strategy and encourage the development of people, client, and firm.	
7. Give productive regular feedback and feedforward on each piece of work. I don't bottle all criticism up until appraisal time and let rip.	
8. Communicate inspirationally, appropriately, and effectively.	
9. Regard everything as a learning opportunity to develop.	
10. Monitor, measure, evaluate, and take remedial action where necessary on all strategy.	
11. Manage poor performance productively and immediately with evidence.	
12. Agree unambiguous and genuine deadlines. I always ask first and mutually agree date, day, time (which time-zone), quantity, and quality. False and artificial deadlines generate mistrust and cynicism.	
13. Am consistent in dealing with people and situations.	
14. Manage difficult people constructively.	
15. Resolve conflicts.	
16. MBWA – manage by walking about.	
17. Deal with issues before they become crises.	
18. Lead by example.	
19. Take clear and decisive decisions with appropriate timing.	
20. Follow-up everything: everything I ask anybody is done to deadline. If a deadline is missed, I follow-up and help the individual to take action so it does not happen again.	
Total	

150-200: Your firm/department/team is united in its direction and moving forward with your leadership, support and example.

100-149: Your firm/department/team knows where it is going and can develop further. It will do well but will need to concentrate on methods, follow-through and flexible adjustment.

50-99: Your firm/department/team are doing well but you may need to clarify direction and method of getting there. There is huge potential to develop. There are great creative ideas, but concentration may need to be given to developing them and implementing them consistently.

The quiz above gives the key managerial and business traits that you will need to be a great partner. Let's pick out a few of the key requirements.

Delegation

This is key to the development of a partner. Unless you can delegate effectively and efficiently, it will not be possible to carry out all other responsibilities.

You need to ask with every job in future, "Should I be doing this?" You should not unless you are making decisions, inputting authority, or adding value that no one else can. You need self-discipline to hand over work that you really like doing but could be done more cost-effectively by somebody else.

There are two ways of delegating. First, telling the person what you want to achieve and detailing how to do it. If they follow your instructions, then you will receive what you anticipated – as long as they understood your instructions. The second way – which is more time-consuming but more beneficial to all in the long-term – is to say what your objective is, and then allow the person to go away, think about it, and come back to you with their structured ideas and timing on doing it. This method can be repeated in small blocks so that you can monitor and tweak the process throughout, keeping control of the work. The result is that it develops the person, and they may come up with a completely different approach, which is different and even better than yours.

Monitoring regularly does not mean micro-managing. If a partner receives a piece of work, and then gives no feedback but starts to re-draft or correct in detail, there is a risk that those people working for that partner will not put too much effort in because they know it will be changed and any issues or mistakes will be picked up by the partner. This leads to, "Why bother? They will correct any errors."

Feedback

Feedback is essential on every piece of work done for you, in order to grow and develop the individual doing it. The partner must start from the perspective of the person to whom the partner has delegated, at each stage of the delegation process. The partner can then understand the delegatee's thought processes, approach, strengths, and weaknesses. Feedback must always start from the other person's perspective first.

Rather than making a statement or judgment, ask a question. The partner should not start with, "This is wrong. That was a bit stupid, wasn't it? That was the wrong way to approach it. There are lots of spelling errors in it. This is rubbish." (It has been known.)

For example, these questions are useful:

- "What were you trying to achieve?"
- "How did you approach it?"
- "What were the difficulties?"
- "What do you think is good?"
- "What do you think you could do better?"
- "How could you approach it differently in future? What else?"
- "What lessons have you learned?"

Tip: do not be afraid of silence. If the lawyer does not respond as quickly as you like, don't answer for them. Wait, patiently. After you as the partner have exhausted all these questions, you can start giving your feedback. Feedback must also be part of regular one-to-one meetings with each junior lawyer.

Appraisals or performance reviews

These must be part of this regular one-to-one management. Appraisals are essential. They must be meaningful, have a clear objective and structure, and the partner must give them time. They must not be canceled or postponed. Lawyers have sleepless nights before an appraisal, and canceling or postponing it says, "We do not value you and your future".

Poor performance

Dealing with this requires courage. If all the approaches above do not produce the desired results and the performance of the lawyer is still not matching the KPIs or standards set, then it is essential the partner deals with it immediately in a systematic and structured way.

People recruitment, retention, management, and development

These are an essential part of being a partner. For many, this is far from being a lawyer. However, a partner must deal with any "people" issues immediately and a partner must not bury their head in the sand and hope that problem goes away. If nothing is done about an obvious people problem, the rest of the team may become demotivated, perceiving favoritism or that poor quality work and careless administration is acceptable. This may ultimately lead to mistakes being made or good people leaving.

Financial management

This is a key requirement of a partner. It is covered at a strategic level in chapters nine and ten. Here I am considering it from a managerial aspect. Many partners really do not like talking about money, generating bills, or chasing them up. This dislike is contagious and may permeate down through teams to individuals.

Accurate time-recording is vital to the overall calculation of how long work and matters take. Disbursements and expenses must be accurately recorded and receipted. This must be ingrained from the first day a lawyer joins the firm and followed-up constantly. If any lawyer is not doing all these speedily, accurately, and consistently, then the partner must notice and take action to ensure that it happens in future.

Many lawyers find it embarrassing to quote fees or ask for money. Money on account for fees and disbursements helps cash flow. Lawyers should role play with other lawyers being difficult – quoting fees, negotiating discounts (not just giving them away), asking for money on account, and chasing up unpaid bills. This benefits both sides of the role play because it enables the person being the prospect or the client to understand their perspective by acting it.

Bills must be issued regularly, as agreed with the client, and not allowed to accumulate, generating shock and anger, as the client receives a huge bill, unexpectedly much higher than anticipated. A little and often helps with the client's financial planning and the cash flow of the firm.

When quoting for a matter, credibility is undermined if a fee or hourly rate is quoted, and a discount immediately offered, without being asked for. Alternatively, if you give a discount just because somebody asks, without taking a little of the service away, it looks as if you were "trying it on" in the first place. Be proud of, and believe in, the value of what you offer.

Dealing with issues to prevent them becoming crises

Introducing new policies and ideas means that risk assessment and management is another key area for managing clients, the firm, teams, and individuals. Partners must identify the risks, assess their likelihood against impact, and take appropriate action – reducing it, sharing it, transferring, dealing with, or not doing it. Many firms have risk departments but a partner must be acutely aware of risk at all times. Any new strategies, approaches, policies, or ideas should be given to an objective, analytical group of critical thinkers to pull apart or improve. This requires courage and confidence on the part of the partner but avoids being single-track minded; it avoids "group think", it can generate new ideas, and it can prevent unintended consequences.

Personal traits of a partner

Partners need empathy, self-awareness, and emotional intelligence to understand their own reactions and their impact on others, whether clients or colleagues. They also need self-discipline. Self-discipline requires the self-motivation to do what you ought to do as promised, and not be driven, as perhaps you were in more junior days, by threats, fear, or deadlines. It requires the self-discipline to take action when you do not feel like it (for example, dealing immediately and objectively with difficult situations or people) and the self-control to stop, or not to do or say something.

Partners need to be consistent, be fair, be seen to be fair, while at the same time being flexible.

Below is a checklist to fill in and from which you can develop a personal action plan to help you develop the characteristics of a great partner.

Trait	Out of 10 1 = low/poor 10 = high/ excellent	Target mark	What I am going to do to achieve it
1. I am good at being non-judgmental and not jumping to quick conclusions by understanding the background and context.			
2. I acknowledge that I am not always right.			
3. I acknowledge and take into account that everyone does not think like me.			

continued on next page

Trait	Out of 10 1 = low/poor 10 = high/ excellent	Target mark	What I am going to do to achieve it
4. I actively look for ideas/opinions that are different from mine and may be better.			
5. I actively try to avoid "group think".			
6. I am always open to new ideas.			
7. I try to learn how others think: clients, colleagues, team members, those above and those below me.			
8. I deliver on what I promise: I am trustworthy and reliable, am honest and have integrity.			
9. I do not say anything negative about anybody to anybody else.			
10. I have a positive and constructive approach.			
11. I take a genuine interest in people; for example, remember their names and what they have told me.			
12. I look for solutions, not problems.			
13. I regard problems as challenges, not obstacles.			
14. I am objectively realistic but not pessimistic.			
15. I don't interrupt or finish people's sentences. I don't assume that I know what they are going to say.			
16. I regard everything as an opportunity.			
17. I learn from everything – even the worst.			
18. I incorporate learning from challenges and am not overcome by them.			
19. I ban the word "they" from my team because it is generally about blaming others.			
20. I aim to be respected rather than liked by my team in my role as their manager.			
TOTAL			

As a partner you need confidence, not arrogance. I have prepared ten steps to C-O-N-F-I-D-E-N-C-E below.

Confidence comprises four elements:

1. Emotional: E
2. Intellectual: I
3. Body Language: BL
4. Dress and appearance (although you may think they shouldn't, people make judgments): D.

Step		Tip	Comment	Element
1	C	**Chant** to yourself: "I am great. I can do it. I will do it."	Say this smiling, with power, and you will automatically feel more confident. Chant when you feel low, threatened, challenged, or overwhelmed.	E
2	O	**Others:** Imagine that everybody knows you are outstanding.	This applies: when you are about to go into a room, meet a difficult client, give a presentation, do a piece of work, be interviewed. In other words, anybody you ever have anything to do with.	E
3	N	**Negativity:** Dismiss all negative thoughts immediately. Go back to Chant in 1.	Ask yourself, WIIFM? (What's In It For Me?) to think negative thoughts about myself. Answer: nothing. Make sure the people around you are radiators, not drains: they radiate positivity rather than drain your resources!	E
4	F	**Face and body:** Much of the way we communicate is through body language. It is two-way – your emotions and thoughts can affect your body and your body affects your emotions and thoughts (e.g., sad thoughts can make you cry).	Eyes – look people in the eye. Smile (appropriately) – even if alone. It will make you feel confident. Three deep breaths in through nose – out through mouth – deep into your tummy. Head: look directly at people and nod when listening. Keep shoulders down, not near ears. Back straight. Hands: move to give voice range and timbre, but not above shoulders or too distracting. Hands: control them: don't fidget with face, hair, rings, pens. Open arms and wrists when asking questions. Feet firmly on floor (appropriately). Exercise will make you feel more confident.	BL
5	I	**Initiate** ideas, projects, plans, activities, actions.	Generate and inspire action.	I

continued on next page

Step		Tip	Comment	Element
6	**D**	**Dress** appropriately, always.	Check your appearance from head to toe frequently. It should make you feel good and inspire confidence in those you meet and with whom you work.	D
7	**E**	Be **Enthusiastic**	It is catching. It inspires others and their reaction will make you feel confident in yourself. Use positive words and phrases. Avoid negatives.	E
8	**N**	**Notes:** • Situation • Your action and reaction • Outcome • Your evaluation (see 10 below)	Keeping brief written notes will enable you to watch your confidence grow and monitor your upwards progress.	I
9	**C**	**Curiosity:** This is fundamental to confidence – to take the focus away from you.	For example, if someone is negative, hostile, and makes you feel undermined, then be curious as to why. Use open questions: 5 x W – Who, when, where, what, and why? 2 x How: How? How much?	I
10	**E**	**Evaluate:** Everything you do (however disastrous in your perception) positively and constructively.	• What did I do well? • What could I have done differently? • What lessons did I learn? • How will I apply these lessons next time?	I

With strategic, leadership, managerial skills, and strong personal traits, you will be a great partner.

Chapter 6:
Relationships are (the) key to a successful and fulfilled career

By Paul Williams, managing partner, Denver office, Shook Hardy & Bacon

How many times have you heard someone say, "It's not what you know, but who you know"? Sounds simple enough, but let's break it down. What you know matters a lot because unless you are knowledgeable and effective in your field and win the results that clients require, you will not become the trusted advisor that clients call when they need help, no matter who you know. Junior lawyers are confronted at the beginning of their career with the reality that what will set them apart from another is the time they invest in studying and doing. This work effort accumulates experience and propels professional growth during their career. Junior attorneys generally learn to do this "what you know" part of the equation quite well. But as these lawyers mature in the practice and begin to consider whether to pursue partnership in their law firm, they raise their heads and see that they are surrounded by other talented lawyers who have also worked hard and invested in professional development, each of them also winning the opportunity to play on our ultra-competitive playing field. So how does a lawyer win promotion to partnership, and how does a client select a trusted advisor from this crowded field of talented attorneys? At this crucial moment, having already established oneself as a capable competitor who can get the job done, "who you know" now matters a lot. And who you have cultivated and developed a meaningful relationship with matters the most.

Many junior lawyers have accompanied mentors to a client meeting or social gathering and heard story after story about past events. Those events may have occurred in law school or in the early days of professional careers, and they certainly include deals or cases through the decades that were hard fought and won. The stories reference legal matters, but almost always include reference to social and personal details, too. By observing the mentor and client interact, the junior lawyer senses the confidence, the depth of trust, and the personal nature of the relationship – a closeness that transcends the evolution of company ownership and changes of employment. The junior attorney begins to realize this visit is not really about the new assignment. This visit is about nurturing the relationship – as evident from the welcoming, familiar hug when they greet each other and the warm smiles as they each share about their family and current home project. The junior attorney nearly forgets about the PowerPoint so meticulously prepared for the meeting. What matters now is absorbing this moment to try to learn how to develop what is being eye-witnessed – a meaningful relationship between a lawyer and a client, an authentic friendship.

Relationships provide a source of work, which is good for business, and can help support a bid for partnership in your law firm. Whether you want to be a partner or not, relationships provide a woven connection between who we are and what we do as lawyers. Being a trusted advisor is not a job, it's a privilege. We don't punch a clock, we live a profession, one that should be filled with purpose and happiness. Relationships are (the) key both for business (which leads to promotion and greater compensation) and for purpose and fulfillment in our chosen career. If you appreciate the attributes of these kinds of relationships, you likely are not surprised that these relationships take time and require constant attention year-round, not just at holidays or when convenient. But authentic relationships feel natural and are fun. They won't feel at all like work. And everyone can have them if they commit the time and invest in the effort.

How you get there will be tailored to you. There is no one-size-fits-all instruction guide for building relationships. Everyone will have their own style and their own way, but there are two key elements to put into practice that can make a substantial difference in your relationships. The first is to be yourself; the second is to be available, and make time for people.

Your way is your way, and it will likely be different from others, but should be true to you. Do not confine yourself to repeating how others have gone about it. Instead, evaluate the options and find what works best for you. Absorb tips from mentors and employ suggestions from others in the practice to find and refine your style and your way to create connections and develop relationships. If you want to become a partner, ask questions of those who have become a partner about their path. What worked for them? What's most important in their relationships? And what lessons did they learn in the process?

If you invest in yourself and in developing relationships, you should be able to make your own connections and develop meaningful relationships with others. Relationships lead to business, and business leads to partnership. And, hopefully, you will have the opportunity to enjoy the privilege of being a trusted advisor to one or many clients as well. You have made it this far; you can take these next steps, too.

Where do relationships begin?

The first step in the process of developing relationships and winning new business is to learn and perform the substance and practice of law. There is no way around it. You must master the fundamentals of the legal profession and demonstrate proficiency and efficacy – win client-favored results. Every member of the bar is permitted to do the work. What stands out are results, how you obtained those results, and the client's overall experience. Were you attentive, knowledgeable, experienced, and responsive? Did the ultimate cost align with the risk and outcome? Did you do all you could to manage the matter and achieve the best outcome possible under the circumstances, and does the client know that without you having to say anything about it? Trust is the core building block for relationships.

Not every case is going to be a win (as in, an all-or-nothing, winner-takes-all verdict that trial lawyers want for a "win"). Did you talk about what a "win" looks like, and did you meet or exceed the client's expectations for a win? Did the outcome help accomplish the client's business and legal objectives? And if not, by knowing the client's business and the impact of the outcome, you should provide a plan and offer next steps that will turn the loss into a win. Not every case is going to be an all-out win; in fact, you may experience a shocking loss. In those instances, what you do next and how you do it matters the most.

But it is here – in the trenches, working alongside your colleagues and the client team to prepare and present matters – that you will begin to shape your professional self and clients will begin to develop impressions of you as a lawyer and as a person. These impressions will evolve over time with further interactions and additional shared experiences. The collective exposure sets the stage for what comes next.

The cultivation of relationships – mutual respect

Whether described as admiration or awe, trust or faith, at the core of a desirable relationship is a mutual understanding and belief that each of you is good for the other and that each of you adds value to the relationship. Respect is not automatic. It doesn't come with a job or with a role. Whether a junior attorney is working with a senior partner or with a client, it is just as important that the junior and senior respect each other and the client as it is that the client respect the senior and the junior. And everyone needs to be respected by the Court, and show respect. Mutual respect is earned through dedicated work and committed effort, and also by attention to the individual – the person – not just the role. Timely updates and responses to colleagues and clients and a proper tone in communications are also critical. (Caution:

do not sacrifice tone for the hasty speed of a response.) Respect is delicate, and requires focus, tending, and thoughtful care. Respect takes considerable time to build, little by little, and a misstep can exponentially set you back. Depending on the severity of the setback, rehabilitation can be even more difficult than the original effort. Mutual respect is a treasure – nurture and guard it and it will be the building block of many good things to come.

To illustrate, in our profession one way respect is manifested is in the quality of the work product we provide. This is an area where "going the extra mile" makes a material difference. A brief may include arguments that are clear, concise, and well-phrased and be just fine. But if the brief were to also include a segment illustrating the argument to make it come to life and a footnote to distinguish a contrary authority, and perhaps a graphic to visually demonstrate the concepts, now the brief resonates and conveys a depth of knowledge and application of the legal principle as well as credibility and appeal as the most-correct interpretation of the issues. The additional detail also aids the decision-maker (the client or the judge) in assessing the alternatives and making a decision. That extra effort may make the client's position before the court more compelling and the desired outcome more likely to be achieved.

For another example, if you know your client has a report-out session with a "boss" every week, provide an easily digestible status update with talking-point highlights to facilitate your client's internal report-out. It's easy enough for you to do and even if your client already knows what's going on, the organized format and timely delivery makes your client's day a little easier, the report-out to the boss go a little quicker and better, and the client's (and the boss') overall experience more positive and beneficial to the relationship. Even if your update goes to the senior partner and then to the client, the effect is the same and you have nurtured both your relationship with the senior partner and with the client.

You also show your respect by meeting (and beating) client deadlines. Clients are incredibly busy. Often they do not have time in their schedule to take lunch or go for a refreshing walk, let alone schedule a call or review a lengthy email late in the day attaching a 30-page brief with even more pages of exhibits that you want to file in the next few hours. Plan in advance and deliver work product early (or at least at the agreed time). Establish a reputation for being prompt on delivery and for doing what you say you will do. Clients (especially those with global responsibilities) have to work extra hard to have some sense of work–life balance and that challenge becomes even greater if your communications are frequently after hours. You want to be on the "nice" list, not the other list.

As you might anticipate, with mutual respect comes more opportunities. A job well done means another job to do. And again, and again. More opportunities also mean more experience learning and doing the things that we do. And with all that experience, your senior partner (and the client) want (need) you in the room. And that is where it happens – where high-level information is shared, where strategy is formed, where decisions are made. Being in the room is a vital part of the transition from associate to partner. That is also where you learn more about the company, corporate personalities, organizational dynamics, and external factors unrelated to but very much impactful to the matters at hand. You also begin to learn more about the client, professionally and personally, and how the matters impact the role, the client, and their future. Chances are, you likely will learn more about your senior partner, too. But these are the early steps you want to be taking to position yourself for partnership, and these are the interactions that will deepen your relationship with the client (and your senior partner).

The power and privilege of relationships

You may wonder what the benefit is of having relationships with clients. In addition to the economic benefits of business generated that is credited to your name at the law firm, which is helpful in a track for partnership, consider your own personal relationships – with a parent, grandparent, sibling, friend, teacher, or mentor. These relationships have provided critical guidance, offered emotional support, and helped you overcome obstacles that at the time may have seemed insurmountable. These people have tangibly contributed to your success so far and many likely continue to do so, even if indirectly. Relationships can be powerful, memorable, life-changing, and lifelong.

The same can be true in our professional lives. Consider those things you do daily in your practice and reflect on why you do them the way you do. Work vigorously to help, to solve problems, to advance projects, and to win results for clients. Provide a draft document on time (or in advance) so the client has plenty of time to review. Meet with the client and roll up your sleeves together to dig through documents and details and interview witnesses to determine a strategy or a solution among challenging options. Consider the scope of your interactions, too. Over time, more and more work events are combined with social events. You thoughtfully attend to the little things for a client meeting to make your client's travel a little easier, a bit less burdensome. Perhaps you receive a telephone call that your client's company has just been acquired and your client needs help finding a new opportunity. More frequently, status calls become as much or more about updates on the family and discussions of summer travel plans and favorites of all kinds (restaurants, books, places to go).

When work life blends with personal life, when clients become friends, when relationships evolve to helping the person (in addition to the company) with professional as well as personal challenges, you have a closeness you can feel, a connection that is far more than that of a procurement department and legal services vendor, and a special bond that provides benefits for, but way beyond, the business.

Tending to avoid mending relationships

As we all know, relationships take time to develop, and if harmed, they can sometimes be difficult to repair. Respect, trust, confidence, and the continued relationship itself depend upon thoughtful and constant attention. It's a two-way street, no question, but you should plan to take the lead. Keeping in touch is paramount. On the legal matters, naturally, but also on life. It's not small talk – it's sharing. It's not a waste of time – it's the best use of your time. The legal work will get done, but the emotional response to the interaction after the Zoom call has ended or the meeting has concluded depends on how the work is done and the "look and feel" of the interactions along the way. Those regular updates previously mentioned or timely sharing of drafts so they don't land on the desk after hours are two examples of how to do it right. Being available, which includes being responsive, is vitally important. Taking the time needed to share, as well as to do the legal work, is critical. To evolve a relationship requires sharing. To nurture a relationship requires time for sharing. And to successfully grow a relationship requires an in-the-moment connection while sharing. That sharing happens on Zoom calls, in texts, or by email sometimes, too. And it for sure can happen in-person in and around case or project events if you plan for it (and make time for it). Time is valuable. We know it, and clients know it too. Give freely of your time – your non-billable time – to create and capitalize on moments of sharing. Your client will appreciate it and your relationship will grow.

Keeping in touch does not always look the same. Sometimes it is a text or a call. At other times, it may be an interim update on a recent case opinion, or a notice of appeal in a competitor's case on an issue of importance to your client. You should put yourself in the pathway of information that educates you and keeps you informed on matters of interest to your client and the company, and then share information from your feed that impacts the company. Perhaps it is sharing a copy of a company press release that hit the news, or a complaint you see come through from an unsatisfied customer on the internet. Perhaps you have learned of a plaintiff's class action firm soliciting for information about your client or a product or service they offer. Or you can share a heads-up on a new law that passed that may impact compliance. Adding value beyond the work you already provide is, well, valuable. As you learn the business, pay attention to and share information and insights about the business. The interim updates provide you with additional touchpoint opportunities, and your client will appreciate the thoughtful attention. You may also identify additional opportunities to help support the company and your client through new work, areas of work, or new practice areas (creating an opportunity to introduce your client to colleagues at your firm).

Hands down, though, in-person shared experiences are the best. There is no lost time in a day together. It's great to meet for coffee or breakfast before the day begins. Then walk or ride over to the meeting. The meeting is the meeting, but in and around the meeting are more opportunities for sharing. You can have a quick side conversation on the events in the meeting and preview options or suggested next steps, or even provide a quick update on a different matter or share a photo posted by one of the kids. Perhaps you can share a heads-up about a new development to talk about after the meeting, or check in on plans for dinner and maybe introduce them to someone new before you go. Whether the event is work-related, a hybrid work-social activity, or a dedicated social event, time together is invaluable. In work mode you do your thing – prepare to meet any challenge, and in doing so provide the best representation as your client expects. In non-work mode, be attentive to the person and to the relationship. You check in and ask them how they're doing, are they comfortable with the direction, and whether everything is landing as they had anticipated. If any adjustments are needed, outline the alternative steps ready for the taking if those steps better meet the need. You are the rock, the advocate, the sage, the communicator, the whisperer, the confidant, and the solver. That's what we do, and how we do it matters to the relationship as much or more than the actual outcome. The look and feel and the emotional response after the event has concluded matters – a lot. Until you connect again, that takeaway – that snapshot – is stored as RAM memory of the shared experience. You want to be sure it positively reflects on the relationship, as well as the event, in order to preserve the progress you have made in cultivating the relationship. A legal win for a work event sure helps, too.

It's not too late to identify and build relationships

Each of us has the ability to identify, cultivate, and develop meaningful, lasting relationships with clients. And if you desire to become a partner in your law firm, having your own relationships, which leads to your own business, can move you forward in your path to partnership. Not everyone's situation has provided the same opportunity, but you can explore a path to find your way. (If the obstacles are too great where you are, you might consider evaluating alternatives to create a situation that will support you building your own client relationships.) Even if you have not yet begun the process, it is easy to get started.

You first need to take stock and make an inventory. Ask yourself (and make notes):

- What do you do?
- What industries are you involved with and what businesses do you know fairly well?
- What types of matters do you manage and on what issues do you offer counsel and advice?
- What's your niche?
- What other activities do you do – community, professional, hobbies, and otherwise?
- What is your passion?
- What makes you excited to learn and read, and what makes you excited to talk about and experience?
- Who do you know in each of those areas and activities?

Sketch these thoughts into a flow diagram and evaluate how they interconnect. Now consider the same thoughts in a Venn diagram. Look again for the connections. Don't be discouraged; it's a point of beginning. Add the names of your friends and colleagues to the diagram. Identify others you can talk to about the activities and talk to them. Add their thoughts to the diagram as well. What stands out to you as your greatest connection(s)? Brainstorm the opportunities and identify the warmest, most resonant connections by name (along with their industry and business). This process can help you identify a place to invest your time and attention. If your focus is an existing client relationship, talk to your partner with the client relationship and ask how you can be part of the relationship and help grow the business (and in turn establish a succession plan for the business). If it's a new relationship, talk to your mentor for support to get started, make a plan and reach out to the client. Now is the time to be brave and to stretch yourself beyond your comfort zone.

Part of your outreach plan should include a review of what additional efforts you can make to place yourself in the pathway of your priority opportunities. Identify the organizations or industry groups that support the industry or business. Establish a pipeline of information pertinent to the industry or business to be alert to trends and changes that may impact your contact in that industry or business. From your study and preparation, you can identify possible gaps in service or a new need on the horizon that you can provide. As a hint, take a look at what's happening with the company's competitors – often what impacts one impacts many. You may obtain some insights on what your contact is dealing with or potentially facing down the road and can offer strategic insight and support so they are ready when it comes.

Although you may be working to develop your first client and your first relationship, be sure to check with your network. Yes, you have a network. Perhaps it is mostly family, friends, peers from college or law school, or colleagues at your current firm, but ask around. See who they are connected with on LinkedIn and what organizations and groups they follow. See who the partners you work with are connected to and be sure to connect with your partners on LinkedIn so you see what comes in their news feed. Observe what kinds of information are positively reacted to and evaluate what you may have in your experience from work (or otherwise) to share. Generate content. Post and share. And if the insights are tailored (or tailorable) to a contact, industry, or business, share it with your contact and others in the industry and business directly (in consultation with the relationship partner if he or she has an existing relationship). Talk to your firm's marketing team, too. They likely will have good ideas for you on how to most effectively reach contacts and clients and share helpful alerts, insights, and substantive content.

But do not fret. It's not too late. The investment of time and effort will be worth your while. Having one (and, even better, six or ten or 20) robust client relationships can be as liberating as it is rewarding in your career and in your professional (and personal) life. Having relationships and business can be the difference-maker in your candidacy for partnership, and will enhance the character and quality of your professional career. And kudos to you if you are privileged to connect on a deep level with client(s) and become a trusted advisor – to be that person the client calls for anything and everything and with who you are able to share your practice and your life. Talking daily, working daily, enjoying life daily, and looking forward to tomorrow. Find purpose and happiness in what you do. It's possible, it's rewarding, and it's fun. Plus we get to make a living doing it, too.

Chapter 7:

The importance of relationships – the seven pillars of development

By Pippa Blakemore, The PEP Partnership LLP

The ability to create, build, and maintain meaningful relationships is fundamental for those looking to become a successful partner.

This chapter identifies the seven essential pillars of development:

1. Understanding the importance of strong relationships.
2. Knowing with whom you should build and maintain durable relationships.
3. The mindset that lawyers need.
4. Principles needed to progress from associate to partner.
5. Where to build relationships to strengthen your future when you become a partner.
6. Appropriate communication.
7. How to turn contacts into a loyal client base and a strong book of business.

This chapter aims to confirm what you are doing is right, to introduce new ideas, give tips on how to make what you do most appealing and effective, give advice on how to motivate yourself, provide tips on how to make the most of every opportunity, and highlight traps to avoid.

Understanding the importance of strong relationships

Lawyers must build strong durable relationships, because their contacts, clients, referrers, and intermediaries are "buying" a lawyer or a team of lawyers. Lawyers are not selling a cold, measurable, machine-manufactured product. They provide advice based on sound judgments and relevant experience, so that all partners, lawyers, and attorneys, at whatever level, are an integral part of the service provided. Ultimately, the objective of building relationships for those looking to become a successful partner is to build a book of business, to be a work winner, and to build and grow a client portfolio as discussed and developed in chapter eight.

Many lawyers find the following structured ideas abhorrent and say, "I did not become a lawyer to be a salesperson". I agree totally.

Others have said, "But it is all so false. It is artificial and insincere. Everybody will see through it." Here, I disagree.

On both counts, if a partner, or an aspiring partner, is an excellent lawyer, supported by an outstanding team, within a superlative firm, then that attorney is letting down everyone with a legal need if they do not ensure that they, or their firm, or others they know and trust, help such an organization or individual.

Much of what follows is "common sense". That's true. But what matters is implementing it, rather than just knowing it. An additional challenge is that relationship building gets submerged beneath the demands of chargeable work, high pressure current demands, and short-term daily crises.

The increasing use and impact of AI makes strong personal relationships even more important.

Knowing with whom you should build and maintain durable relationships

Current clients

In many law firms, work and income from current clients makes up between 60 and 80 percent of annual billing. It can cost up to 20 times more to win work from new clients than to win work from current clients.

Current clients have to be nurtured, especially long-term ones. Relationships may become too familiar and clients may feel that they are being taken for granted. I know of one partner who missed a deadline for a client of many years, saying, "I'm sorry that I did not do that for you, but I was working hard on pitch presentation and just didn't have time. I know you will understand." That partner was surprised when this long-term client was poached by another law firm.

Nurturing current clients to generate repeat business is easier in some practice areas than in others, for example in corporate, real estate, and employment. In other areas, for example family and a once in a lifetime divorce, where legal advice is a distress purchase and nobody wants to see a lawyer again, it may be more difficult.

Current and past referrers, intermediaries, and ambassadors

Where repeat work is less likely to be generated, it is even more important to build meaningful and mutually respectful relationships with referrers, intermediaries, and the firm's ambassadors.

Ambassadors of the firm are those who praise the firm and its lawyers to their wide network of friends and contacts, enhancing brand profile and creating opportunities for introductions and referrals. Recognition and acknowledgment is an essential part of cementing relationships.

This is important from the moment you enter the firm, so that as you progress up the firm towards partnership you have developed relationships with those more junior than you and your peers. As you progress up the firm, they too will progress up their corresponding organizations, so that when they can give you work, you are able to receive it as a partner.

Past members of the firm

These may in future be a source of work, whether in-house or at another firm, where they may pass on work if conflicted out, or do not have the resources or lack the necessary specialism. If your peers leave, keep in touch with them, and let them know your progress to partnership, in order to generate mutually reciprocal referred work.

The mindset that lawyers need to progress from associate to partner

Perseverance

Developing a relationship into work can occasionally be very quick but can take many meetings and communications. It may take up to ten or 15 contacts over several years. It is the long game.

For example, going to a conference, seminar, or business event, and being expected to come back with work is similar to going to a party, looking around, going up to the most likely prospect, having a chat and then saying "Will you marry me?". Just like personal relationships, business relationships take thought, time, and perseverance.

ABC – Always Be Curious

Understand your current contacts, prospects, referrers, intermediaries, and clients comprehensively. For example, learn, understand, and discuss their vision, mission, objectives, needs, priorities, problems, pressures, and the issues they face. Study their environment, context, and industry. Monitor what they are doing and with whom they are doing it, and how successfully. This is where AI can be hugely helpful, taking the time and drudgery out of such research.

If you are already working for a client, don't assume anything. Keep checking their preferred way of working and what they want, need, and require from you. Monitor changes in their organization and change the way you structure your team and service to reflect this if necessary.

One lawyer (who confessed to me and said I could tell his tale) who had done some drafting that he was really proud of went to a client meeting and for two hours went through this wonderful 60 pages of advice with the client. At the end, the client sat back and said, "All I wanted to know was 'Yes' or 'No'".

If the contact or client is open to it, the lawyer can also take an interest in the joyful and happy parts of the lives of the people they meet – their families, hobbies, activities, aspirations, and dreams.

ABE – Always Be Enthusiastic

An attorney, particularly associates aspiring to be partners who are the future of the firm, must be committed to and passionate about their own work, describe it with enthusiasm, and identify how it helps and has the potential to help others. One law firm went to a beauty parade. They were the preferred firm. But the partners and associates who were also on the presentation team because the clients wanted to meet those who would be doing the work, were not enthusiastic about the potential client organization or its objectives. They did not say that they really wanted to do the work or ask for it, and so it was awarded to another firm.

Be alert to opportunities to help

Lawyers should constantly look for ways to help or enhance the lives of others. But not in a pushy way. For example, if someone you are talking to mentions a question or challenge, then you could offer to help or to put them in touch with somebody they know who might be able to help. This may range from the legal to the personal; for example, the person you are talking to mentions they are going on holiday to a certain place that you have been to. You could suggest a special restaurant, walk, or place to visit. Or, if someone has been injured by over-exercising, you could suggest a good sports therapist.

Constantly check on needs, requirements, and expectations

The most useful five "open" questions are Who, What, When, Where, and Why? There are also two Hows – How? and How much?

Open questions plus superlatives, such as "most," "best", "greatest", and "largest" generate the most information. You can make it sound less like an interrogation by using preliminaries to soften the questioning.

- "I am really interested in understanding your priorities. What's the most challenging issue you face now?"
- "Last time we discussed your strategic plans, you mentioned that X was the biggest problem you face. How much has that changed?"

Feedback at the end of a matter is essential. But do not send a form or allow others to send a form for feedback on your behalf. It belies that you have a close personal relationship that the client might have thought you have developed over the matter. If the form takes too long, you might find yourself with a bill for completing it from the client, based on your hourly rate!

Feedback must be done personally, preferably face-to-face, or via video call, because it gives you an opportunity to find out the future plans of the client – including their strategy, vision, mission, objectives, and targets – and enables you to identify how you can help in future.

If you are not yet a partner, but were involved in the matter, ask to be involved in the feedback discussion. It will help you understand the client better and prepare for future dealings with them.

Approachability

Try to look at everything from the other person's perspective. I met one associate who said that they always use Latin when writing advice and talking to people because it made them look clever. An eminent surgeon, at the top of his field, said that he always felt a fool, small, insignificant, and nervous in meetings with lawyers.

Listen – with your eyes and ears and check understanding

We have two ears and one mouth. People only hear about 20-30 percent of what is said to them. If it is something bad, then it may only be five percent or less. Therefore, you need to check constantly that anybody you are talking to understands what you have said. For example, sometimes people use legal jargon but do not understand the legal implications of what they are saying for fear of looking stupid to the lawyer. To avoid this, you can ask a client to summarize what they think you have said. Similarly, you can summarize back to a client what you think they have said. The other person just has to reply "Yes" or correct it with "No, this is what I said or meant".

Check that the body language matches what the other person is saying. For example, they might be saying "I agree" but if they scratch their neck, put their hand over their mouth, don't look you in the eye, or start to turn away, it indicates that they may not or that they feel uncomfortable about it. Use open questions to find out what they really think and feel.

I worked with an associate who said that he had to talk because that was what the clients were paying for. He talked a lot. I suggested that he be quiet. He was very hesitant. I met him a couple of weeks later, and he told me that he had let the client talk for an hour and 20 minutes. The client then said, "That was the best meeting I have ever had with you".

Principles of nurturing relationships

Strong relationships develop from like, to trust, to entrust.

Change "I" to "You"

Change your focus from yourself to the other person. For example, if you are tempted to talk about yourself, change it around and ask a question about the other person. Change the wording from "I", "Me", "Our", and "We" to "You" and "Your". For example, if you are asked, "Why should we choose you?" answer, "Because YOU are … and we would like to help you achieve that".

The three-step approach on which to develop long-term relationships requires the following:

- *Hook:* anything you talked about, which will enable you to make a …
- *Commitment:* a suggestion that you make in order to help and keep in touch, with …
- *Permission:* essential so that it does not feel "cold" and that the contact is expecting it and has agreed to it.

Where to relationship-build to strengthen your future when you become a partner

Internally downwards – with your staff, departments, and teams

Strong relationships in this direction will bring out the best in everybody, so that the individual, the team, the department, the practice area, and the firm give the best possible legal service. In addition, if any of the members of the firm leave – either for other firms or companies – they can become invaluable referrers, if they have had good relationships built on respect and trust.

Internally across the firm – to nurture close-to-home referrers

Systematically visit all the other departments in your firm. Don't say, "I want to come and tell you what we do". They won't necessarily want to listen. Ask to attend internal departmental meetings so you can understand more what they do – listen to their pressures, priorities, and issues. Find out what you can do to help, how you can ensure that you understand their position so that you can refer work to them and, if you already do that, how you can make their lives easier in your joint efforts to work together.

Give other departments "trigger" words, so that if they meet anybody who has need of your services, they know what words to listen for. Even if they do not know anything about it, they know that you do and so can refer the person to you.

You can also ask them for "trigger" words for their practice area, so that you can refer people to them.

If you do this as an associate and maintain this after you have become a partner, you will build strong relationships over time, which will help your transition to partnership, and strengthen the firm and increase the quality of the service it provides to clients.

Industry and sector organizations

Join local, national, and international general and specialist legal organizations and networks. Get involved in these not because you are more comfortable talking to other lawyers, but rather because people you meet will be able to help you, your clients, and your contacts.

Join your clients', referrers', and intermediaries' generalist and specialist sector and industry organizations, so that you can learn about their approach, vision, problems, pressures, influences, and factors they need to consider. You can learn their vocabulary, understand their jargon, and use it authoritatively. This will enable you to offer more in-depth practical advice based on in-depth knowledge of their industry. AI can help hugely in the research required.

Starting as an associate means that when you reach partnership you have a strong network of contacts at all levels in relevant sectors and industries. You will also have an in-depth understanding of the context in which they work.

Everywhere and with everybody from the moment you leave home

In any practice area you are in, it is important that you start building your network from school, through university, on holiday jobs, from law school, in your neighborhoods, through your hobbies, interests, activities, and socially.

Talk to people – on planes, trains, at coffee. At conferences and seminars, sit in different places throughout the day. Ask well-informed questions at seminars and conferences, so that people know you and will come and talk to you afterwards, giving the opportunity for relationship initiation. You can start doing this as a junior attorney.

Every time you meet someone is an opportunity to start building relationships. Even if no work arises, directly or indirectly, then at the very least you can have a great conversation and extend your knowledge. You never know where these may lead.

How to strengthen and deepen all relationships:

- One-to-one meetings and/or smaller group meetings.
- Teach-ins or workshops or seminars – that you are giving or tailored for the prospect, referrer, client, or for the industry.
- Send a personal, relevant email, WhatsApp, Facebook post, or post on X (previously known as Twitter) or on Instagram, concerning something that will help them.
- At your own firm's seminars/presentations/workshops/events/ receptions/ activities invite other individuals in your firm – not as 'fillers' but personally and by a formal invite.
- Offer to speak at conferences. These must be where your clients/potential clients or referrers are or are likely to be.
- Aspire to chair conferences – where your clients, contacts, or referrers are likely to be.
- Build relations with the media, so that they will come to you for a comment, knowing that you are easy to talk to, responsive, and understand what they are looking for (within firm policy and take professional training first).
- In addition, publicize your successes. Within the bounds of confidentiality, share your successes with everybody. People like to be associated with success. Again, do this within firm policy and take professional training first.
- Analyze what those people with high profiles are doing and learn from them.
- Make sure that each event and activity you attend has three distinct parts – planning beforehand, your activity during an event or activity, follow-up – systematic, informed, patient, personal, and persistent without being pushy or irritating.

- Invite representatives from clients at the corresponding level to you, to present at seminars/conferences. Invite to small, specific, targeted, imaginative events (originality may count more than cost – clients do ask whose money you are spending, if it is very extravagant).
- Invite to lunch – themed/targeted/with people who would like to meet each other. (Tip for when you are a partner: the higher the people in the organization, the less seminars appeal. They do not feel the need to learn anything. They feel they should be presenting at them.)
- Invite to dinner/opera/concert/running training.
- Invite to a sporting event, e. g. golf, cricket, rugby, the races, football, hockey.
- Secondment.
- Shadowing.
- Activities with your peer groups, from university, school, hobbies, clubs, and activities.

Appropriate communication

Methods

Use the method that the contact or client prefers. Many lawyers now say that much of their communication is by WhatsApp. Do not do what is most comfortable for you. Don't always write because that is what is easier for you, and gets it off your "To Do" list. Ask those with whom you are communicating, and use their preferred method.

Frequency – other person's perspective

This depends on what you agree with the person with whom you are building the relationship. Always try at the end of each communication to agree (if you are talking) or suggest if you are writing, the next time you should be in touch and the method to use and the day, date, and time and who initiates.

For example, at the end of an email with advice, instead of writing, "If you have any questions, please do not hesitate to be in touch," replace this with, "As agreed, I will call you in two days' time to see if you have any questions".

This means that you do not feel it is a "cold call" or that you are intruding because it has been agreed.

Many times, when the lawyer telephones a couple of days later, after the client has been grateful to the lawyer for being reliable, answering their questions, it has been followed up with, "While you are on the phone, could you just do this for me, as well?"

It is important to remember this, because too often the feeling is that once you have sent off the advice, you can move on to the next task because it is no longer your responsibility.

Keep in regular touch, even when you are not billing. This demonstrates that your business relationship is genuine, even if you are not being given work. One general counsel told me that it was really annoying only to be contacted alongside huge bills. Another firm lost a large, long-term client by not keeping in touch for two years when they were not billing them. When the next huge matter arose, the client gave work to a new firm that had been nurturing the relationship for two years with no return.

Content should always answer "WIIFM?"

Make every communication personal – business or not – and valuable to the person with whom you are communicating.

The subject heading in an email should always answer WIIFM (What's In It For Me) in order for a person to open it and to read it. In WhatsApp, the first five words can be read without opening the message, so make those five words the key points of the message.

If you start your WhatsApp with "Hi [name], I hope that you are well", there is a possibility that it will not be read any further. The receiver may say to themselves they will read it later and your message will slide down the received messages, totally off the screen by the end of the day, to be lost and forgotten. Then you might get annoyed that they do not reply.

A really good check for sending relevant information is to ask the question, "So what?" and adding the statement to the communication, "… which means that you …" and adding why it is relevant.

If you cannot answer "… which means that you …" on the recipient's behalf, then either double-check their needs or don't include it.

Don't just necessarily send information about their business. If you are communicating with an in-house team in a specialist sector, do not send them information on their sector, unless you have discussed that it would be useful.

One general counsel told me that he knew far more about his own sector and industry than any private practice law firm. What he wanted was information about areas that he did not have good experience in, for example, property and employment. But he was never asked by any law firm what would be most helpful to him. He was simply put on mailing lists for his sector.

How to strengthen and deepen communications:

- Highlight relevant parts of an article you have read that might be of interest.
- Approach (with permission) with business opportunities from another client, contact, or referrer.
- Be alert to opportunities for reciprocity.
- Look out for changes in the prospect's or client's organization.
- Communicate changes in your firm, as well as changes and developments in what you can offer.
- Let someone know when you have met a mutual friend.
- Share proprietary research of yours.
- Mention, in plenty of time, seminars you are organizing and/or speaking at, as well as seminars/conferences you are attending.
- Do the same with social events you are organizing or attending.
- Tell people when you have been promoted or have worked on something recently that might be interesting.
- Congratulate your contact or prospect who has been promoted.
- Be aware of announcements of a company's results. Watch the share price.
- Keep abreast of anticipated changes and current changes in the political regime, as well as changes in competition/competitors/industry of the client's organization.
- Discuss changes in environment, changes in their market, and current court cases.
- Understand implications of changes in legislation in their jurisdiction, as well as legislation in other jurisdictions (e.g. the US, Europe) that might have implications for them. Keep on top of legislation in your own jurisdiction.
- Monitor general press and/or media coverage of their organization.
- Arrange to discuss when their organization has reorganized, or if there have been recent events or activities in their organization.
- Communicate recent judgments, recruitment drives, tax changes, changes in regulatory framework – indeed, anything that might affect their business or organization or that might be of interest in view of their interests or hobbies.

Volume

Make it short and relevant. If, for example, there has been a change in the law, or a recent case or matter of interest, don't send a long document. Send three or four bullet points in an email or WhatsApp, all of which answer the question "What's In It For Me?" Only include what will be helpful and will take their business forward or enhance their lives.

Assume that nobody reads anything, and that people do not click on links or open attachments. This will enable you to be the most helpful to them. It will allow you to be concise, succinct, and impactful. In-house counsel may have 50-100 matters to deal with at any one time, all over the world in different time zones.

Sending newsletters, Facebook posts, and LinkedIn alerts about your own firm does not necessarily build relationships. Sending self-congratulatory newsletters about a lawyer's own firm and its internal partying activities does not build relationships. Some clients receive up to 500 emails a day and more than 150 newsletters from law firms a year.

Sharing personal successes on a one-to-one basis, in a brief personal message, can be most meaningful.

Frequency

Little, often, and consistently. Relationship-building is difficult to fit in when you are busy. It is easily identifiable by recipients if you only get in touch when you are not busy.

Try to spend a quarter of an hour per day, which is one-and-a-quarter hours per week, which is 60 hours in a 48-week year. In other words, almost a working week.

Tip:

- Set an alarm to start and an alarm to finish.
- Time record it.
- Monitor progress each week and each month.
- Be systematic and responsive, personally and regularly, according to each individual.

I know a hugely successful lawyer who spends half an hour every morning, first thing, telephoning contacts, clients, referrers, and intermediaries, following up and finding out how they are doing. He has a constant stream of work.

Be systematic and organized

Whenever you have had a conversation or communication with a person, and when it has gone from the business to nurturing the relationship, then there are six things that you need to record (subject to all data protection laws). These are:

1. Date.
2. Method of communication.
3. General information, e.g. hobbies, interests, families, schools, holidays.
4. Hook – generated from what you talked about.
5. Commitment – any follow up action that you promised to take and when you said you would do it by.
6. Permission – have you put in your calendar to do what you said you would in accordance with the client's consent?

Follow-up is absolutely critical. It shows:

- You mean what you say.
- You are reliable.
- You care.
- You are organized.

How to turn these contacts into a loyal client base and a strong book of business

Relationships are the foundation of a strong book of business and a loyal client base. Nurturing your clients, ambassadors, referrers, and intermediaries is essential over the long-term. This is covered in much more depth in chapter eight.

Two key tips are:

- Recognize the "closing" signals – i.e. the signs that a prospect wants to give you work.
- Always be enthusiastic about everything – others and yourself. Ask for the business.

Build the seven pillars, slowly and enthusiastically, on strong foundations and your relationships will grow from strength to strength preparing the way for you to be a successful partner.

Chapter 8: Business development for the aspiring partner

By Tom Bird, bestselling business author, trainer and keynote speaker

It's fair to say that most lawyers did not join a firm in order to become a salesperson but, as you progress through the ranks, the role of business development (BD) becomes increasingly important. There are a lot of misconceptions about what BD is for a lawyer, what it involves, and the attributes necessary to be successful. The reality, however, is often a relief to lawyers. Most highly effective work winners don't feel that they have ever "sold" anything to anyone in the conventional sense of the word; they have just had some really interesting business conversations and formed some mutually fulfilling business relationships. Fundamentally, BD success for you is about being authentic – being yourself but with a little more skill. In the absence of an innate motivation around BD, the key requirement is for you to have focus and discipline. The focus to ensure you spend time on the right things and the discipline to do it regularly.

In this chapter, we will look at what the very best work winners do and understand how this can be personalised by you to guarantee success in the long game of BD without having to change your personality. We will recognise that there are challenges but give you clear priorities to ensure that you move the BD aspect of the role forward.

The context of BD for an associate

When you are newly qualified, almost all of your focus and time is spent on learning your technical craft. As you progress, other aspects of the role become visible – you are exposed to the wider practice, to client meetings, to supervising and delegating to others and, of course, to BD. The reality is that as each of these transitions emerge, you have to carve out time for them as an individual in an environment where you are always busy "doing the work". In a very real way, BD is a choice that you make and every choice has consequences. The positive consequences of engaging with BD include more choice over the work you do, broader and more fulfilling relationships (both internally with colleagues and externally with clients), and a significantly higher chance of being considered for partnership.

As an associate within a firm, there are lots of interferences that can, if you let them, conspire to reduce either the amount of BD activity you do or the effectiveness of it. Let's look briefly at a few of these.

Mindset

Your mindset will either support or detract from your commitment to engaging in BD activities and the results you achieve. The best mindsets to support BD, present in all highly effective work winners, are confidence and curiosity. But for a lot of associates, your sense of confidence is linked to your feeling of competence. When you feel competent, perhaps technically around the work itself, you are confident, but if you are put into a different situation where you may not feel as competent, your situational confidence reduces. One consequence of this reduction in confidence might be to ask questions to which you already know the answer so that you can feel safe that you are able to contribute. The best work winners, however, are comfortable asking questions they do not know the answer to, and this sets them apart as their conversations are broader and more client-focused as a result. There is no change without self-awareness and so taking stock of how confident you are in a situation will enable you to take action as and when you need. By shifting physiology or doing some mental rehearsal/visualisation (which all elite athletes do, for example) of an upcoming meeting or other BD situation, you can have a positive impact on your situational confidence. The reality is that you create deeper levels of confidence by "practicing at the edge of discomfort" – the same way you have learnt any important skill you have developed!

Lack of time

The day job will always be demanding and many associates question how they can find enough time to dedicate to BD activity. The reality is that highly effective work winners have the same challenges and yet they manage to carve out time each day to spend on BD – and they ensure they spend it on the right things. If you can dedicate even 15-20 minutes a day, most days, for BD activities (and assuming you spend that time effectively) it will make a difference and will help set you up to succeed in the long-term.

Limited contact with decision makers

It may be that most of your contact is with members of the in-house client legal team rather than the senior people who make the decisions around awarding work. This is true for many associates, but the reality is when we ask most partners to track back their best client relationships, they often find that the relationship started before they were a partner and before the client was in a position to award work. By doing the right things with our existing contacts – both within our firm and within client organisations with whom we work – we build a foundation for winning future work.

A partner who may not support your BD activities

Not all partners are collaborative or proactively supportive of your BD efforts and if you work for one of this sort of partner it can be difficult to see how you can move your BD efforts forward. However, no one will be more interested in your career than you, so you have to take individual responsibility to commit to actions that you do not need permission for, which can build up your BD skillset and effectiveness. The priorities discussed later in this chapter are examples of these types of action.

What clients want over and above the work – the starting point for any BD

"People buy people" and they tend to make a decision emotionally and then justify it logically. If we are to differentiate ourselves in a crowded market of legal technical experts, we have to deliver against more than just a client's legal technical needs.

We have already mentioned that BD is not a "pushy" act of selling. When your technical knowledge is the "product", if you are felt by the client to be selling to them they are likely to respond negatively. The most effective work winners seek to influence rather than sell; they seek to really understand a client's needs and add value in any way they can (and not just through their own practice-specific legal technical knowledge). UK-based research (conducted by the PSFI) shows that, over and above the work that professionals deliver, clients are looking for three key areas of added value. Understanding these areas will help you focus your activities in order to build personal value and differentiation in the relationships you form.

A curiosity in the business and the sector

Potential and existing clients experience business issues – not legal issues. Whilst the law might be their way of addressing these issues, they need to feel that you understand, and are focusing on, what's at stake from a business perspective. Being curious about a particular business and the wider sector that it is part of, the trends and challenges faced and the business value of the work you seek to deliver, are all important potential areas where you can positively differentiate. This requires you to prioritise checking their website, reading around a sector etc. in order to inform the questions you ask and the way you frame and articulate your legal advice.

Access to an integrated firm

Over a period of time, the legal needs of a client are likely to be much broader than just those addressed by your own practice specialism. Clients want to have access to broader expertise as and when the need arises, and they will look to you to field the right people at the right time. Again, your curiosity, this time combined with a broad and relevant internal network, will support you in differentiating yourself from other firms and individual lawyers.

A focus on the right kind of relationship

Clients are looking for lawyers who focus on building a specific kind of relationship. Yes, they expect high levels of availability and service delivery, but these alone are unlikely to differentiate you. They want you to put the relationship first, partner with them, be good with their internal managers, and understand their needs as individuals as well as a business.

What is helpful here is that none of these three areas require you to "sell" in any overt or pushy way; they simply require you to focus authentically on what's important to the client and, in so doing, you make yourself more attractive and differentiated compared to other lawyers.

Key priorities for associates

With the context you have as an associate within a firm, and in light of what we know clients are looking for from the professionals they work with, we can define some key personal priorities that, if you focus time and attention on, will ensure that you are making the very best use of the limited discretionary time you have available for BD. As BD is a long game, you need to invest some time in each of these personal priorities regularly if they are to pay off. The good news is that by creating daily BD goals that should take less than 15-20 minutes to achieve, you make real progress over time. In each of the areas that follow, think about some 15-minute actions you can take and get into the habit of doing one action each day.

Build your profile

If you want to attract the right connections and build the right relationships in the longer term, you need to have a profile that speaks to who you are. This is likely to see you positioned as more than just a narrow legal technical expert; as someone who is interested in the client's business and sector. There are a number of small, practical steps you can take to help build a great profile.

- *LinkedIn:* It's important to engage with platforms such as LinkedIn and be proactive in posting and commenting on other people's posts. When you do this, look to have a view, link to other information, and resist the urge to simply regurgitate messages from the firm. Have your own voice, comment on industry sector trends, ask questions, and engage with posts from other people.
- *Attend events to grow your knowledge.* Think about sector-based events that you can attend to build out your knowledge of the issues, challenges, and opportunities that exist. This wider sector and business context will enable you to have wider conversations with the people you meet and help change their perception of you as a narrow technical expert in your practice area to someone who is interested in and knowledgeable of the wider sector.
- *Report internally on developments in a sector from the perspective of your practice area.* To help build your internal profile within your firm, recognise that the experiences of clients around your practice area might be of interest and value to other fee earners and partners in your firm across other practices, giving them a wider context for their work. The more you are known by, and know, fee earners across practices in your firm, the more likely you are to get referrals. Again, being seen by these colleagues as having a wider sector and business interest will help create the right perception.

Architect your network

Highly effective work winners recognise that their network is critical and they build it out in a thoughtful and proactive way. They look wider than just the obvious contacts (people they have worked with, colleagues in the firm etc.) and look to make connections across a sector that are relevant to their clients, not just from a legal perspective. These might include referrers, finance specialists, consultants, advisors, and industry bodies. Their approach to forming these connections is often through questions about a sector or examples of how they have helped solve a current sector-based business problem for a client.

They also prioritise building out and collaborating with connections in their internal (firmwide) network – cross practice and cross office. There is a lot of compelling research about the personal benefits of doing this in a professional firm setting with direct links between the degree of internal collaboration between lawyers and the resulting revenue streams.

Another characteristic of the best work winners is they proactively look for opportunities to introduce people in their network to each other. If your network (both internally and externally) is broad, there will be lots of opportunities for people in your network to benefit from, or add value to, others in your network. This proactive thought about making connections between people is a natural habit of the best work winners.

There are two concepts that underpin how you need to approach every aspect of your networking – reciprocity and leveraging weak "bridge" connections. By recognising and leveraging these concepts you can dramatically change how you feel about networking and the results that you achieve from it.

Reciprocity

Reciprocity is the well-proven concept that adding value to someone sets up a tension whereby they want to repay that value to the giver. In networking terms, work winners naturally approach all their networking through the lens of seeking how they might be able to add value to that person. They recognise that the people with whom they network are individuals with individual challenges and so the value they give is personal to them rather than "firm to potential client organisation". As soon as they meet someone, they are thinking about how they might add value to that person. The pay-off from this approach is substantial. Firstly, it can change your perception of networking from a "selling" opportunity to a "giving" opportunity. From conversations with highly effective work winners, about two-thirds of the people you give something of value to will repay it in some way. This might be through an introduction or some information that you can take to others to bring them some insight or value. Of these two-thirds, some individuals will pay back the value received exponentially.

When you approach all networking with reciprocity, it means that any conversation with anyone new to you (whether or not they are involved in anything to do with clients in your sector) is an opportunity to seek to add value. All of this enables you to leverage weak "bridge" connections, which is one of the secrets of attracting work.

Weak "bridge" connections

Most of us have networks that comprise people we have known for a while, maybe from university, law school, clients, and colleagues we have worked with. These long-lasting connections are often helpful but will not necessarily result in us winning work directly. Often, work givers in client organisations network with a different circle of people that we might not know ourselves. By using reciprocity with everyone we meet, even those with whom we only have a relatively fleeting contact (so a "weak" connection), we still set up the conditions whereby that person wants to repay us for the value we have given. So when they go back into their own long-term network, they will potentially recommend us if someone they know has a problem they think we might be able to solve. Think about yourself – if you have ever needed a one-off product or service and you felt you received great service or good value, you want to recommend the supplier to other people who you know. It's the same contact.

Partners who are great at BD nearly all reflect that they get phone calls from people they have not met themselves and do not know that often result in work. This is a result of using reciprocity and leveraging weak "bridge" connections.

Track the winners

If you ask a lot of partners to track back their best existing client relationships to how they began, they will often say that it started before they were a partner and before the contact was in a position to award work. The reality is that a number of the in-house teams you work with now will have individuals who will go on to be the work givers of the future. If you think about it, you probably have an idea already of who they might be. There will be individuals you work with now across your clients who have ambition, seem to be moving forward, and are likely to be the work givers of the future. By making objective choices to spend time with those people, you can invest in those relationships, seek to add continuous value, and stay in touch so that as they progress and you progress, the relationship pays dividends for both parties. It is all too easy to spend time with people we like the most or have easiest access to, but by being a little more thoughtful about our choices we can make better use of our limited time.

Having the focus and discipline to take small actions around these three priorities each day will build the foundation for your future BD success. If you consider these three areas alongside the previous section of this chapter, which looked at what clients want from their lawyers over and above the work, you will see that the theme of relationship runs through everything. There is a very specific kind of relationship that the best work winners form with their internal colleagues and clients that differentiates them from being considered only as legal technical experts. It is this we will look at in the following section.

What is the "right" kind of relationship to build?

Chapters six and seven both have relationship as their focus and you will find some overlaps here. This is because there are some clear relationship dynamics that contribute to positive differentiation, where part of your objective is to be seen as more than a legal technical expert alone.

Let's look first at how a new relationship develops with a potential client, following an initial introduction. After an initial introduction you might have a first meeting where you have been called in to look at a particular issue the client faces, which your practice can help solve or address. The meeting might focus on the specifics of the issue they face and involve you asking questions to find out more about the issue and then credentialling yourself as a lawyer best placed to help them. You can imagine in this situation that your conversation focus is about the specific issue and the value you bring is primarily in terms of your legal technical expertise. Whilst this is natural and in itself not an issue, it can support you being seen by the potential client as the "expert for hire". The challenge with this perception is that there is no shortage of legal experts for hire in the market and so it a) makes it difficult to be seen as differentiated from other lawyers, and b) can limit the value a potential client thinks you can bring to just your practice area specialism. Our objective with every relationship we form (and this goes for internal firm relationships as well as those with external contacts) is to be differentiated from other lawyers by both our ability to add value through more than just our practice area expertise and to understand and be able to discuss the wider context of the clients' needs and challenges. In other words, how do we move from being perceived as an "expert for hire" to being seen as a "trusted advisor"? As our relationships are formed through conversations, we need to consider the specifics of these conversations and how we can manage them to create a differentiated view of us.

Research into client/professional relationships by Andrew Sobel (see Figure 1) provides us with a simple but powerful model to consider for every conversation we have. There are two dimensions that we can focus on in our conversations to help create a differentiated, advisor-led relationship and some specific things we can do by way of our planning for these conversations to be best placed to deliver on these dimensions.

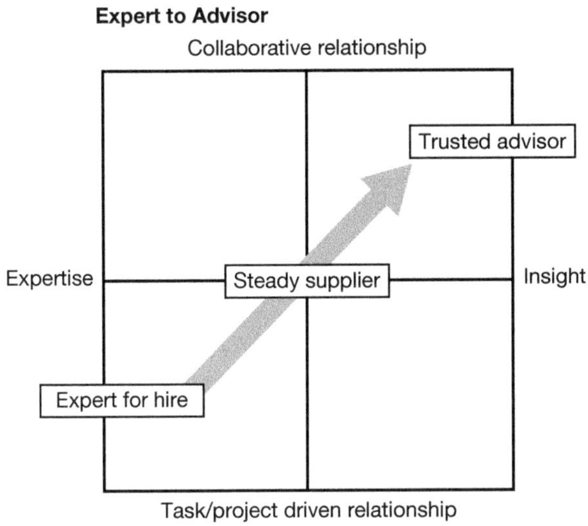

Figure 1: Expert to Advisor. Source: It Starts With Clients, *by Andrew Sobel. http://andrewsobel.com/*

Focus of the conversation

To move up the y axis on the model you are looking to gain greater context from the client rather than focusing exclusively on the specifics of the presenting issue you are discussing. You are looking to find out information such as "Where does this issue sit relative to the other business imperatives of the business?", "What other aspects of the business will be affected by this issue?", "What are the future trends and priorities that the business is thinking about?" etc. In order to be best prepared to move up this y axis you need to a) make time in your client meetings to have these broader discussions and b) plan some questions that you can ask to help create this dialogue.

Remember what we said earlier in this chapter – one of the success factors with highly effective work winners is that they are comfortable asking questions to which they do not know the answer. Your clients know that your focus is on the legal technical issues, but they want you to be curious and they want advice that addresses their business problems so it's important to make time and plan questions. One highly successful firm, from the perspective of client relationship development, challenges its partners to spend 30 percent of meeting time with clients discussing "off-matter" topics and they do this to help ensure partners move up the y axis.

Delivery of value

The x axis of the model is about where you seek to deliver real value to the client. It is relatively easy to remain in the position of delivering value solely through your legal technical expertise and, whilst this expertise is important, it can limit you to being seen as only being able to add value here. By asking the right questions and by being well connected internally and to the issues and trends affecting a sector, you can deliver insights. Remember, your clients are often in an environment where they are acutely aware of the issues they are facing but less aware of what's happening to other organisations in their sector and what specific issues others are facing. If you can bring broader information, that you often take for granted because it comes to you through the work you do already with other clients or the conversations you have across practice with other colleagues, this can be seen as insights by the client. If you are delivering insights in addition to your practice area legal knowledge, your relative value to a client increases.

We have said that the best work winners don't feel that they sell; they just have interesting business conversations. By following this model and adopting the same view, then every conversation is a BD conversation because it represents an opportunity to build this kind of differentiated work-winning relationship.

As we have mentioned before, developing your skills in these areas requires you to practice at the edge of discomfort – particularly when asking those broader questions around the client's business that might be outside of your area of specialist knowledge. By taking these steps, knowing they are stretching your comfort zone, you will find it easier to plan and ask the right questions and gain confidence in knowing that you can bring insight to the people you speak with. Curiosity is the supporting mindset for both of these conversation dimensions.

The Sobel model helps you focus on the right aspects of a conversation to help position yourself as an advisor rather than an expert. It is worth mentioning, however, that your progress towards that goal of being seen as a trusted advisor also requires the client to want to see you in that position – you cannot force it. Your ability to build person-to-person (rather than simply expert-based) trust contributes to your success and should be a priority with both potential clients and existing ones.

Your business card and qualifications will bring a level of professional trust, but it is important to build personal trust and to consciously build on this as the relationship develops.

David Maister has researched this area as it relates to clients and their professional advisors. In his book *The Trusted Advisor*, Maister identifies four components of trustworthiness – credibility, reliability, intimacy, and lack of self-interest. See Figure 2.

The Trust Equation

$$\text{Trust} = \frac{\text{Credibility} + \text{Reliability} + \text{Intimacy}}{\text{Self-interest}}$$

Source: The Trusted Advisor, *by Maister, Green and Galford, Simon & Schuster Free Press, 2001 and 2021.*

Most lawyers pride themselves on their credibility and reliability, which is to do with service delivery. But these two things alone are unlikely to differentiate as *all* lawyers working for a client are likely to score high on these components. The real opportunity for building a differentiated level of trust is to build client intimacy – your knowledge of the client's business-related issues and their individual, more personal, situation. By growing this dimension of your knowledge over time through asking the right questions, you build trust and a relationship where you can add broader as well as more personal value to your clients. This requires a conscious effort to progress your conversations as research shows a lot of lawyers stay more focused on the more obvious business-related issues and do not develop the conversations to identify more about what the individual needs are (career aspirations, current challenges etc.) where you might be able to help and add value.

From everything we have covered in this section of the chapter you can see that the right kind of relationship is something that should feel congruent and authentic to you. Most of us want to add value to clients and, once we know how to do this, we should feel comfortable stretching ourselves to deliver, particularly as this does not involve overt "selling".

There is one other area where you can support your development and success in long-term business development, and that relates to setting the right kind of goals.

The role of goal-setting in BD

You can only manage what you measure, and you can only measure what you monitor, so if you want to manage and develop your BD effectiveness you need to set some goals. But business development differs from the work product delivery that you are used to. Whilst there are likely to be goals around revenues, share of wallet etc. there are also going to be other goals relating to relationships that are less tangible and longer-term and it may be less obvious that you have achieved them. Your daily efforts and activity need to be focused on doing the right things even though you may not see immediate, tangible results.

In his book, *The Seven Habits of Highly Effective People*[1] Stephen Covey says that "the main thing is to keep the main thing the main thing" and that is certainly true of business development. You need to regularly engage in the right profile, network, and relationship-building activities and it helps to set some goals to encourage you to do this. We have mentioned one professional service firm that targets partners to spend a minimum of 30 percent of meeting time on "off-matter" conversation. This is a helpful goal to focus your discussions on building broader context. That same firm also uses a 2-4-8 approach for managing a business development pipeline – each partner should be engaged in two active projects, seek to have four proposals being developed, progressed, and discussed, and be engaged in eight broader conversations that may lead to a proposal. This metric focuses the mind on ensuring you have sufficient activity across a sales cycle to avoid the "feast or famine" situation that many professionals experience.

What goals can you set yourself around business development that will support or progress to results? Drawing again on the work of Stephen Covey and our research into highly effective work winners, effective BD goals have the following characteristics:

- There is a big picture objective that connects to your motivation, the "Why?" this is so important. This defines what you are looking for in the longer-term. This might be a revenue goal, a number of new clients, positioning yourself as the "go to" person in a particular niche etc. When you are busy and not feeling particularly motivated, having this big picture objective can help engage you in taking action.
- Activity-based goals are important. Whilst BD is about relationships, profile, and how we want to be perceived, these are difficult to measure and so we need to create goals that focus on doing the right things, the activities that will move us forward. We have discussed three priority areas that you can build activity-based goals around – building your profile, architecting your network, and tracking the winners.
- The goals you set need to recognise that you have limited time. Make sure that you set goals that will take you no longer than 20 minutes to achieve as you are unlikely to be able to find more time than this

in a day. If you want to achieve something that will take longer than 20 minutes, look to break this goal down into smaller, more manageable chunks. Make sure that the goals are going to move you forward towards achieving a result or building/developing a relationship. This means they are likely to be important and not urgent and so they won't happen unless we prioritise them.

- Adopt a process that enables you to set goals and diarise them each month around the priority areas and check that you have moved forward on the previous month's goals. This links directly to the need for focus and discipline.

Wherever you are on your business development journey, it's important to recognise that success is about being yourself with more skill and not about some change in your personality – there is no one "right" personality for BD success because "people buy people" and so your authenticity is critical. We have shown that the best work winners in law firms have a mindset that is built on curiosity and a comfort to ask questions they do not know the answer to. These foundations and a commitment to focus time on the right activities build long-term success for them. Taking the first step in building your BD plan and success requires some practice at the edge of discomfort but by focusing on developing relationships in a thoughtful and directional way you will quickly find it easier and more natural.

Above all, for most lawyers, BD is a conscious choice in an environment where you are always busy and with limited time. The benefits of taking this choice are significant.

References

1 https://en.wikipedia.org/wiki/The_7_Habits_of_Highly_Effective_People

Chapter 9: Financial management 101

By Tony Young, partner, and Hung Tran, partner, BDO Business Services

There are a variety of aspects to consider when legal professionals begin the transition to partnership. It takes a lot of demonstrated success to reach this level and it reflects a significant achievement. However, the excitement of achieving a partnership role can sometimes cloud the picture around exactly what the position requires.

For the purposes of this chapter, we use the term "partner" in a general sense to represent the pinnacle role in a firm. That is, it could be a partner in a partnership or, where the firm trades through a company, it could be an employee/shareholder.

The move from employee to partner is more than a promotion or excellence in a specific branch of law. As an employee, a lawyer is working for the firm, whereas a partner has a financial stake in the firm and in most cases is the employer. Within this chapter, our advice is tailored towards those with a financial investment in the business and not a fixed entitlement to income.

It is important to recognize that this is an investment. Partners are expected to contribute to the financial wellbeing of a firm, which may entail investing their own capital, sharing in the profits, and taking on personal financial risk. This is a level of engagement that lawyers may not consider when pondering the benefits of partnership.

It's studying those details that will set a partner apart in a positive way and help them guide the business to success. The skills and knowledge that served them so well in earning the appointment – legal excellence, customer service, a proven track record – must be augmented with firm processes and best practices.

Lawyers seeking partnership should go in with their eyes open and a strong understanding of the financial requisites of their new undertaking. They should also be ready to make a financial commitment to the firm, an obligation that will allow them to reap the rewards of success.

Understanding the drivers of the firm

Knowledge of the structure of the firm is one of the most important elements of financial discipline and literacy for lawyers seeking partnership. This knowledge is different to the skills and discipline that has helped a lawyer excel in their individual practice, and will need to be consciously considered prior to partnership. Just because you're good at your discipline does not mean you know the broader scope of how the practice functions or how to run an equally successful practice.

Adapting to the financial aspects of a law firm's operations

Building an impressive resume and history of performance as a lawyer does not necessarily ensure the kind of financial mindset that is required of a successful partner. Prior to becoming partner, lawyers have a relatively simplified workflow, completing jobs as they are assigned to them, logging the billable hours, and moving on to the next matter. The road to partnership requires looking outside of the functional funnel, gaining a different, fuller perspective of the firm's structure and operations. It requires a mind shift change from "doer" to "owner".

When looking to understand the business at large, aspiring partners should consider:

- The client pipeline;
- "Production" and productive time;
- Utilization (the conversion of productive time);
- Conversion of productive time into work-in-progress;
- Billing and collection of recoverable time; and
- Cash flow.

New considerations and priorities

As a partner, you are now responsible for not just yourself and your personal success, but a team and the success of the firm.

Some of the new responsibilities required for success as partner include:

- Finding enough work for all personnel to make the firm consistently productive;
- Converting leads into business;
- Collecting payment in a timely manner;

- Building a strong team of specialized lawyers;
- Minimizing write-offs; and
- Managing outputs on a day-to-day basis.

Some of the financial concepts associated with the partner level can be more challenging to pick up than others. For example, assessing how aggressively to pursue payment from debtors is a nuanced process, but one that partners will have to master to excel in their new roles in driving profits for the firm.

Balancing management with individual work

Partners must adapt more than just their work styles to suit their new management responsibilities. As well as their expanding role in leadership, partners are required to provide work for their employees and secure revenue for their firm, all while finding time in their schedules for their own client work.

It is essential to master the concept of balancing time between producing client work for the firm and managing day-to-day activities. Partners must perform high-level legal work, to the same standards they previously achieved, while also keeping an eye on firm-wide metrics such as:

- The amount of new work and new clients in the pipeline;
- The quantity of work produced relative to team targets; and
- The amount of work billed against budget, along with the percentage recovered.

When these numbers don't meet expectations, the partners must take a hands-on approach to correcting them. Most law firm models require partners to not only be fee-generating, but also fee-earning, which will require them to perform legal work.

Impact of structure

Some aspects of a firm will affect new partners more than others. The structure of the firm is one of many traits that define the relationship between partners and the business. How a firm is structured will impact the experience partners can expect to have.

- *A partnership or trust*. When a firm is organized as a partnership or trust, partners are paid by distributions of profit, which are pre-tax.

- *A company.* In an incorporated company, returns to partners are made as dividends, which come post-tax.

Understanding the structure of the firm before taking on a partner role is vital in order to set expectations. Knowing when and how distributions take place allows partners to make several important calculations, both in terms of cash flow management and the oversight of their personal tax affairs.

Rising from employee to partner

It is important to consider how the status change from employee to partner/owner will impact the individual when making their career transition. This is another case where it pays to understand the difference between partnerships and companies (as outlined above), as the process of moving from employee to partner is somewhat different at each type of firm.

- *At a partnership or trust.* When rising from employee to partner, an individual's tax status changes significantly. The employer – in this case, the firm's partners – is responsible for withholding a portion of each employee's pay for tax purposes. Partners, on the other hand, receive the full pre-tax amount of their pay and must fulfil their own tax obligations.
- *At a company.* The change for employees becoming "partners/owners" is not as drastic in a company as in the before-and-after structure of a promotion at a partnership or trust. The addition of a potential dividend is the primary change for lawyers who become partners/owners at such a firm, while their pay remains tax-withheld. New partners must know what kind of structure they're stepping into so they can understand the impact on their own earnings. From there, they'll have to ensure they have the financial advice to correctly contextualize and manage their new earnings. They should also take advice on how to structure ownership of their new interest in the practice.

Due diligence

One recurring theme for new partners is the need to maximize prior learning to avoid disappointment later. This all culminates in due diligence, the process of appraising what exactly partnership will entail, which must not be neglected.

Being invited into a partnership comes with excitement. This is the moment most lawyers have worked for – a time to start earning profits while also taking more direct control over the direction of their career. Wise partners won't let this anticipation derail their decision-making processes.

Unexpected obstacles – what might unprepared partners discover?

Excitement can lead to hasty decisions and signing contracts without an appropriate level of due diligence. Having signed, a newly elevated partner could be surprised by factors such as:

- *Exposure to liabilities.* Becoming a partner of a firm can mean far more exposure to personal liability.
- *Partner drawing timelines.* The prospect of receiving a distribution or dividend is exciting, but a partner who signs a partnership agreement too hastily may be surprised if that payment doesn't come for several months.

Problems arise from unknowns, whether in general or at a particular organization. With a little planning, it's possible to slip relatively seamlessly into a new role as a partner and thrive financially.

Priority no. 1: read your agreement

The simplest step in due diligence is to read the partnership or shareholder agreement before signing any contracts. The rules, expectations, and norms of the firm are laid out for new partners to read, so they should take the time to do so.

The discrepancy around expectation and reality isn't born out of intent to deceive. Skipping this step is unfortunately common – many newly elevated partners are so caught up in the excitement and anticipation of their new position that they neglect to read their contract or ask important questions. This causes them to have to play catch-up regarding their financial obligations in the months and years ahead.

The value of external advice

One of the best ways to overcome any shock or surprise upon taking on partner duties is to receive an expert opinion on what the contract entails. New partners who run their partnership agreements by a trusted third-party adviser can discover details they may have missed on their own. Seeking a second opinion – from someone who isn't caught up in the excitement of the promotion – can reveal vital details of what will be expected of the partner.

Firm-wide governance and discipline

Employees of all kinds are shaped by their environments. As partners progress through the ranks of a firm, they may gain exposure to financial best practices along the way. A well-run firm is the perfect incubator for new partners, enabling them to come into their leadership roles with a sense of financial understanding and discipline that will serve them well. An environment that fosters a strong regime of financial discipline and governance in place has a positive impact on employees, helping those lawyers who are working towards attaining partner status. It is important to be curious and ask questions.

What a high-performing firm looks like

As with any aspect of business, strong, repeatable, and ingrained processes are important. When a firm is efficient at managing its finances, this trait will form part of the firm's culture. This means employees at every level understand what is required and it becomes part of their day-to-day mindset.

In matters of financial discipline, there are a few specific categories that can set a firm up as a strong performer.

- *Policies and procedures*. Best practices around financial management are reinforced by a firm's official policies around matters such as acceptable levels of WIP.
- *Leadership*. The example set by current partners and managers within a firm determines what is regarded as normal and best practice.

How partners can cope at less disciplined firms

Not every firm has a strong approach to financial discipline and governance. This can be a hindrance to lawyers who rise through the ranks on their way to partner status because they won't learn effective habits.

Aspiring partners whose firms have traditionally not shown strong financial controls must be self-directed in their learning about discipline and leadership. The first step in this process is to look at the firm with a critical eye and decide whether current practices should be maintained or abandoned or even if they should commit to joining the firm as a partner.

How to conceptualize financial discipline

When measuring their firms' current levels of financial performance and imposing their own best practices, partners can make a simple assessment

– does the firm have a responsible approach to collecting debtors on a consistent basis and the conversion of work-in-progress (WIP) to invoices?

It's worth studying up on how a business handles:

- Overall financial management (e.g. does the firm monitor debtor days and WIP days against budget?);
- Budgeting discipline;
- Spending habits; and
- Managing against an agreed budget.

Correct management of working capital

Working capital is one of the most essential elements of financial management for new partners to understand. Many firms are not adept at overseeing their working capital requirements to ensure they are holding the correct levels, so it may land on the partner to pick up this responsibility.

A steady amount of working capital is essential for paying the day-to-day bills at a firm. Everything up to and including salaries must be factored in, and inconsistent or careless management of funds can lead to a feeling of general disorganization and poor management.

Cash flow considerations across firm types

Maintaining an acceptable level of cash and prudently processing cash flow are important tasks that will vary depending on a firm's size and maturity. Specific requirements for cash flow management can include the following considerations:

- Partners at newly founded firms need to think carefully about cash flow management in the early periods. Operating expenses and salaries require cash immediately, but the fees will take time to bill and collect. This timing difference needs to be managed.
- Growth brings its own cash flow demands. Although organizations may become more comfortable operating day-to-day once they're larger, the growth process does require additional working capital.

Cash management challenges for partners

One of the common issues facing firms that don't dedicate enough focus to cash flow management is a constant sense of running low on available working capital. This leads to an uncomfortable feeling of operating "hand-to-mouth" and a need to continually refresh the supply of funds.

Partners will feel the financial impact of such a situation directly because they may be the ones providing the new infusions of working capital to keep the firm operating. By getting ahead of working capital needs, making accurate projections, and preparing for the requirements brought on by growth and expansion, partners will be able to avoid personal burden.

The budgetary discipline and capital management relationship

Many of the issues related to cash flow oversight are tied to the same financial discipline practices and habits affecting overall partner performance. Organizations that have strong policies and procedures in place regarding cash management may set their budgets from 12 months to two years in advance. Detailed budget documents will include cash flow projections, helping partners plan intelligently for the future.

Without a plan laying out priorities and projections, firms can end up operating from one month to the next. This lack of foresight can manifest itself in regular cash shortages, making it harder for the business to focus on its core competencies, invest in important capital projects, or for partners to turn a profit.

Distribution management and policies

Distributions or shares of profit for partners are not handled consistently from firm to firm. Aspiring partners need to be aware of their firm's distribution policy. The ability to pay distributions on a consistent schedule will differ by firm. In ideal conditions, partners will be able to expect an entitlement every month, or every quarter at minimum. This, however, will not apply to firms that lack planning or have lax financial controls.

Distribution management approaches

How do firms react to a lack of sufficient funds to pay a distribution? The answer to this question can speak volumes about the practices and policies in place at a firm. For example:

- Firms that are ad hoc in the way they handle distributions will determine payment based on current financial results, with little indication of what change or action is called for.
- Firms with more stringent financial controls may enact specific policies when income is too low to pay a distribution – for example, setting objectives for partners to clear out their WIPs and collect funds before the next distribution date.

The latter approach is based on greater visibility and discipline and therefore avoids disappointment or confusion among partners. Maintaining alternative plans that can be executed when revenue is lower than expected will lead to a more consistent schedule of payment.

Where budgeting meets distribution

Forward budgeting can also influence successful firm distributions. In addition to containing expenses and projected cash flow, detailed budgets should contain planned distributions.

A budget constructed at least a year in advance lets partners know what's coming and can prevent any big surprises. If the firm consistently hits the budgeted targets in terms of the amount of business won, funds collected, and expenses paid, this will allow the distributions to be paid as expected.

Growth prospects and succession

Becoming a partner isn't just a momentary change. Ideally, a lawyer who achieves partner status will stay with the organization for years to come – guiding it, growing with it, and sharing in its profits.

This long-term engagement demands a forward-looking perspective. When signing a partnership agreement and getting to know a firm, new partners must consider where the business is going, including taking the time to calculate likely future prospects. This means having a clear view of not just the present status of the firm but its trajectory and likely prospects too. Developing such a perspective can seem excessive but will ensure the new partner has the tools to guide the firm to success.

Monitoring growth potential

Is the firm growing sustainably, or does it have attributes that could hold it back? This is something a partner must know prior to taking on their new responsibilities. An organization's current position can indicate its ability to grow. For instance, if a business is tied closely to the clients of a single partner or an industry with uncertain prospects, this reliance poses a clear risk to its future potential.

Similarly, strong present performance doesn't necessarily portend strong growth or the potential for expansion, and this is something new partners should always be aware of. Current success could be dependent upon conditions that will vanish in a few years, be that a personal relationship or a whole industry.

The most prepared firms will have clear predictions about their prospects for continued growth and expansion, as well as plans to fill any gaps. If these don't exist, partners should start building them out rather than running into surprising downturns.

When building growth potential, a new partner can look outside of their own role. Establishing new touchpoints with clients and diversifying their business relationships can drive work in the future. Attracting these types of connections requires partners to know their entire firms and client bases well.

Understanding the firm's succession plan

Law firms are businesses often built on personal relationships. Long-serving partners may have connections with large-scale clients that go back decades and account for large portions of the company's revenue. This system creates potential stressors for future revenue streams. If there is no strategy for when these partners retire, the partners who remain may end up surprised when they are suddenly dealing with a large hole in the firm's results.

Working with partners to introduce new personnel into client relationships and lay the groundwork to retain those accounts for the long-term is important. This requires foresight. After the partners retire, it's too late.

Planning for diversification

Just as a firm can be too closely tied to a single partner's client list, it can also be too dependent on a single industry. This is especially problematic when that sector is at risk of medium- or long-term decline in revenue or overall prominence.

A new partner owes it to themselves and their firm to take a critical look at the balance of clients. If there's too high a concentration of business in one sector, it's wise to have a diversification strategy ready to implement. The firm's future may depend on such a contingency.

Preparation begets success

Becoming a partner involves a new set of financial responsibilities that can be daunting to undertake. Lawyers who take the time to understand the following seven key elements are far better positioned for success in partnership and will save themselves many trials and tribulations down the track.

1. *Drivers.* It pays to know the financial drivers of a particular firm. How does the organization generate its clients? What are its expenses? Are there opportunities to strengthen this picture, and what will the new partner's role be once they're settled in?

2. *Firm-wide discipline*. The financial discipline of an organization may set it apart from less effective competitors. This extends from the practices and policies enshrined in the firm's rules to the actual, day-to-day ways partners and employees handle money.
3. *Working capital management*. Firms manage their money in different ways, with requirements that will differ based on the age and individual requirements of the business. New partners should be prepared to ensure there are consistent, reliable practices in place.
4. *Distribution management*. How are partners compensated for their contributions? Knowing the individual firm's policies when taking a partner role is important to avoid surprises regarding profit-sharing.
5. *Organizational structure*. A firm set up as a partnership will have different rules than a corporation when it comes to the role and remuneration of partners. A prospective partner should know the situation they're entering.
6. *Due diligence*. One of the most common mistakes that gets new partners in trouble is simply not doing their homework on their new role. Reading the contract and researching the expectations and norms of the firm are essential considerations for new partners.
7. *Growth and succession*. How well prepared for the future is the business? Is it being held back by fragile personal relationships or ties to singular industries? These are matters for new partners to study to excel in their new roles and for the future of their firm.

Becoming a partner is an exciting and momentous event. These important considerations aren't meant to diminish those factors, but rather set partners up to thrive in their new role, fulfilling their partner potential.

Chapter 10:
The practicalities and realities of financial management as a partner

By Nicky Owen, partner, professional practices team, Crowe UK LLP

Introduction

When you become a partner in a firm, you really should have an understanding of the firm and how it works. You have an important role to play, and you will be contributing to the financial success of the firm. It is likely that you will be required to contribute partnership capital and take on financial risk; you won't be getting a salary, and instead you will be taking a profit share that may fluctuate from one year to the next and will be dependent on the profitability of the firm.

When you make partner, there is no one to hide behind. You will need to make decisions and take on increased responsibility. Remember, people are now hiding behind you and you are their comfort blanket. Think partner, not employee.

The aim of this chapter is to raise your awareness and help you to ask questions so that you have a better understanding of the financial management of the firm and the role you play within that. Let's face it, if you were asked to invest in a business, you would want to understand that business and what your likely future returns would be. Why should becoming a partner in a firm be any different?

What's the risk? What's the reward? What do I need to know and understand to feel comfortable and confident about asking intelligent questions of management?

Legal background

Becoming a partner means that you will become an owner of the business, rather than an employee of the firm. As a result, you have a responsibility with your other partners towards the employees. A scary thought. Their livelihoods depend on you.

Being a partner will mean that you are no longer entitled to a monthly salary and will instead receive drawings. What level of drawings will you receive, and when are they made? Are any other distributions made during the course of the year? If the firm performs well, you would expect your profit share to increase, but if the firm performs poorly or less well than previously, then you will receive a lower profit share. The security of a monthly salary will vanish. There's a risk.

Moving from employee to partner will mean losing employment protection, literally overnight. How do you feel about that? Do you know what your employment rights were?

Joining a partnership or a Limited Liability Partnership (LLP) (in the UK) will mean that effectively the firm is governed by either the Partnership Act 1890 or the Limited Liability Partnerships Act 2000. The firm should have a Partnership Agreement that you will sign up to. This should clearly set out the contractual obligations that partners have towards the firm and its partners and will provide a framework for the running of the firm. The agreement will cover a multitude of different aspects and ideally should be read from cover to cover!

Do not be afraid to read and ask for clarification on points you do not understand. Partnership agreements should not stand still and should evolve over time and keep pace with life as it is today. A partnership agreement now looks quite different from one ten or 20 years ago.

In a UK general partnership, all the partners are jointly liable for all the debts and obligations of the firm, whereas an LLP is a body corporate and has a separate legal personality to its partners and therefore it is the firm that is liable for all of the debts and obligations of the firm and not the partners.

In the UK, partnerships, including LLPs, are tax transparent for tax purposes and it is the partners that are taxed on the income of the partnership.

Reward

How are you going to be rewarded for being a partner? On what basis does the firm reward its partners?

Firms are all different, partners are all different, so what are the firm's expectations from you? Firms tend to reward on certain criteria or a mix, the likely ones including:

- Work generator;
- Work "doer";
- Technical expert;
- Business manager;
- Growth generator;
- Client handler; and
- Leader.

Do you know how the profits of the firm will be split between partners?

In my experience, I have seen everything from an even split between partners to highly complex calculations based on numerous pools of profit shares that are split on different bases and points – and everything in between.

Some of the ways in which profits can be split include the following:

- Return of capital;
- Base "profit share" for being a partner;
- Equal;
- Lockstep;
- Points system – based on....;
- Performance – based on....;
- Base "profit share" for management roles; and
- High achievers.

The partnership agreement should specify how the profits of the firm will be split, in respect of income. The Agreement should also state how capital profits will be split, which can be different from income shares. This will only be required if a partnership asset (i.e., property or goodwill) is sold to a third party or a fellow partner.

Usually, partners in professional practice firms will contribute capital into the business and, when they leave, the capital contributed is returned. In this case the partners are effectively custodians of the goodwill and do not buy into the business, but they look after the goodwill and grow it and effectively pass the firm on to the next generation at no cost.

However, some firms will trade in goodwill and partners will have to buy in on the basis that goodwill growth will be rewarded when they retire, and a new generation of partners will buy them out.

Partnership capital

It is usual for partners to provide capital into the firm. The firm will use the funds as working capital. It is also usual for partners to borrow the funds, although some firms do request an element of profit share each year to be directed to partnership capital.

Partners will receive tax relief on interest paid on the loan. It is therefore tax efficient to borrow partnership capital.

The firm will usually have arrangements with their bankers for partner loans to be provided for partnership capital and therefore terms may well have already been agreed with the bank, which makes it administratively easy to sort out.

Alternatively, partners can make their own arrangements. However, a partner will have the burden of sorting it out and the terms may not be as competitive.

Statutory accounts

The "stat" accounts, as they are often referred to, are required for LLPs and are focused on the firm as a whole and made up of five key elements:

1. Profit and loss account – this provides details of the profit the firm made in the accounting year.
2. Balance sheet – this provides a summary at that balance sheet date of the firm's:
   - Assets and liabilities; and
   - Capital and equity.
3. Cashflow statement – this provides an overview of how the firm has managed its cash and shows a reconciliation from the opening to the closing cash balance for the period. This statement is often dismissed but can provide invaluable insight into how the firm is managing its cash.
4. Reconciliation of members' interests – this provides a summary of the transactions with the partners as a whole and will include:
   - Movements in capital;
   - Profit for the year; and
   - Drawings.
5. Notes to the accounts – these are supporting information and will include details of the accounting policies and information on specific items in the profit and loss account and balance sheet.

Partnership accounts

There is no prescribed format for partnership accounts; therefore, they are unique in form and content for each firm. You will expect the partnership accounts to be granular and to include individual partner accounts. However, it is likely that junior equity partners will not be able to view all individual partner accounts.

Partnership accounts should include the following:

- Detailed profit and loss account;
- Balance sheet;
- Partners' accounts by partner; and
- Additional notes, likely to include analysis of expenditure.

Management accounts

These are usually prepared monthly for internal purposes; they are a key management tool. Their timeliness is vital, as they quickly become out of date as they are a snapshot of the position of the firm at the month-end date. They will include estimates and will compare actual figures to budgeted performance. A written analysis in relation to key information and trends enhances the benefits of the accounts.

Balance sheet

An example of a simplistic balance sheet is shown in Figure 1. The key point to remember is that it is a snapshot at a point in time, at the accounting year end date.

	2023	2022
	£'000	£'000
Fixed assets	1,120	1,110
Current assets	8,450	7,628
Current liabilities	(1,262)	(1,433)
	8,308	7,305
Provisions	(636)	(570)
NET ASSETS	£7,672	£6,735
Represented by:		
Partners' capital accounts	2,971	2,825
Partners' current accounts	4,701	3,910
	£7,672	£6,735

Figure 1: A simplistic balance sheet.

Fixed assets

These are assets that will be used within the business for a relatively long term or expenditure that will have a long life – for example, leasehold improvements, office equipment, computer equipment, and software. The expenditure is not in respect of "revenue or consumables", which have a short life cycle.

Current assets

These are assets that are either cash or will turn into cash within the year, plus expenditure that relates to a future period.

Working capital forms part of current assets.

There are three key elements of working capital, and they all have a direct impact on cash:

1. Fees that have been raised but not yet paid.
2. Work in progress (WIP), which is where work has been performed but not yet billed.
3. Disbursements paid, not yet recharged to clients.

WIP is valued at its billable value, which will usually decrease in value as time goes on.

It is therefore key to ensure that fees are raised promptly, sent out, and the cash is collected. The longer it takes to issue a fee, the less value there is associated to the WIP. Partners play an important role ensuring that clients are invoiced on a timely basis and that the fee is issued and paid promptly.

Debtors

These are fees that are receivable from clients and will include rechargeable disbursements. It is important that provisions are made for fees that will not be collected, either because they cannot or will not pay.

Raising a bill that will not be collected does not increase profit.

Collection of debts is likely and should be a performance measure.

Prepayments

This is the element of expenditure paid for in the current year, which relates to the next financial year.

Liabilities

This is simply money owed to others and will include products and services received that have not yet been paid for.

Current liabilities

These are debts that the firm owes, that are due to be collected within one year, and will include the following:

- Bank overdrafts;
- Trade creditors and accruals;
- VAT owed to Customs and Excise;
- PAYE owed to HMRC;
- PII claims; and
- Pension liabilities.

Provisions

This is a liability for an uncertain amount, where there is an expectation of a liability, but the quantum is unknown.

Partners' accounts

Capital accounts

This will represent the amounts that partners have contributed into the business in respect of capital. It is a long-term investment in the firm. The amount may vary depending on the capital structure of the firm. Some firms require an increase in partnership capital as you advance through the ranks of equity within the firm. Some will require an element of profit share to be transferred to capital accounts each year. It is usually financed by a loan from a bank.

Current accounts

The account will record:

- Profit shares allocated;
- Drawings paid; and
- Personal expenses paid on behalf of the partner.

The balance at any time will represent the amount that the partner should expect to be paid out at some point. Each firm will have their own policies for distributing profit shares.

Tax reserve accounts

This account will record the amounts:

- Retained by the firm on partners' profit shares to settle future tax liabilities payable to the UK tax authorities; and
- Of tax paid to HMRC on behalf of the partner.

The balance at any time will represent the amount the firm is currently holding on behalf of the partner to settle future tax liabilities.

Profit and loss account

An example of a simplistic profit and loss (P&L) is shown in Figure 2. The key points to remember are that:

- The account shows the results for the particular accounting year;
- There is no standard format;
- Expenses are grouped into categories; and
- There may be departmental analysis.

		2023
	£'000	£'000
Fee income		17,865
Bank interest receivable		285
		18,150
Salaries	10,250	
Rent and rates	1,221	
General expenses	1,892	
Repairs	89	
Depreciation	155	
Entertainment	161	
Professional fees	72	
		(13,840)
NET PROFIT		£4,310

Figure 2: A simplistic profit and loss (P&L).

Fee income

This is the value of work undertaken for clients during the accounting year. This will be a combination of the fees raised plus recoverable work in progress (WIP), work performed but not yet billed.

Salaries

For professional firms, this is the most significant element of costs.

In statutory accounts, this figure will not include any amounts relating to partners.

Management accounts, however, may include a "notional salary" for partners.

Rent and rates

This is generally the second single largest element of expenditure.

Depreciation

This is not a cash expenditure; instead, it is an annual charge designed to spread the writing off of the cost of fixed assets over the period that they will be used within the business.

Management information

At various times you will be provided with management information, and in fact management accounts may well be accompanied by additional information. What does it all mean? Each firm will provide its own information and you are likely to be measured on a variety of them, so if you don't know, ask. There are probably others in the firm who don't know either.

In times of uncertainty, cash is key and management will be looking at how they can accelerate cash into the business. Part of that process is to look at when bills are raised and the likelihood is that your firm's fees raised will look relatively similar to Figure 3.

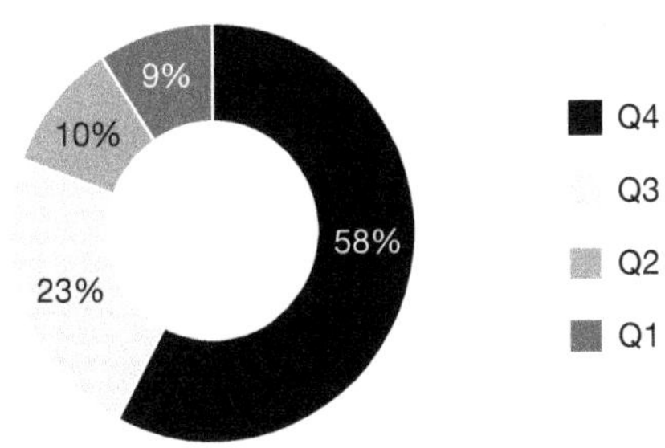

Figure 3: Fees raised per quarter.

What the figure is telling us is that the fees raised each quarter increase as we get close to the accounting year-end. Finance teams will ideally want the fees raised smoothed out across the entire financial year.

Management will also compare departments with each other, so understanding your department's financial management information will help you to understand how your team impacts on the fees raised within each quarter and how your team can make a change. See Figure 4.

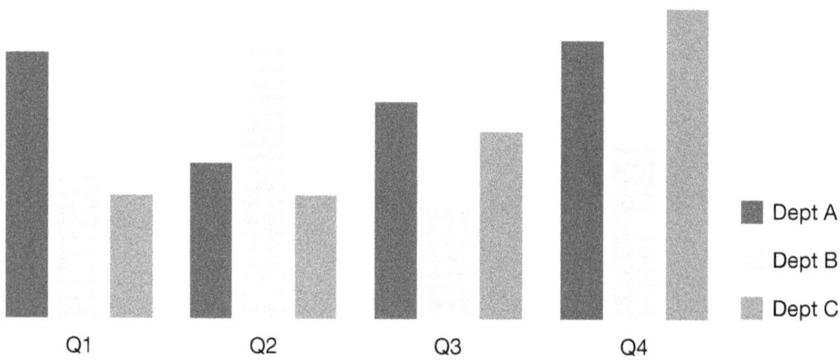

Figure 4: Fees raised per department.

Demystifying the finance

To conclude, I am going to demystify a few terms that you are likely to come across.

Lock-up

This is a measure of work performed not yet collected in cash. It is usually measured in days.

- Debt lock-up is the average length of time that fees are unpaid.
- WIP lock-up is the average length of time from when work is performed to when fees are raised.

Key Performance Indicators (KPIs)

These are the measures that management use to assess performance. They can be firm-wide KPIs and individual KPIs.

Generally accepted accounting practice

This represents normal accounting practice based on accounting standards and issued by a standard-setter. They are required as a basis for statutory accounts and the corresponding tax computations.

However, for preparing partners' accounts, a different basis may be used to ensure and preserve equity between partners and generations of partners.

Equity between partners

It is important that there is a concept of ensuring fairness between partners and considering new partners, retiring partners, and generations of partners.

Summary

There is far more to being a partner than might initially be thought. Partners are, in one regard, guardians of the firm, and it is key that during your stewardship the firm grows and develops. With that responsibility there is a need to have a greater understanding of financial management. This chapter has hopefully provided some insight into demystifying the terms that are used, which will in return give you the confidence to frame and ask questions so that you have a better understanding of how the firm operates financially.

The onus is on you to look at the financial and management accounts of the firm and to understand what they are saying and what that means for the firm and its people.

So often I hear that new partners feel little change in their working lives. There should be, as you are ultimately taking on more responsibility and there needs to be a change in mindset.

Chapter 11: Tax and accounting as a partner

By Nicky Owen, partner, professional practices team, Crowe UK LLP

Introduction

Now you're a partner, the question of taxation looms. Tax may be something you've never really considered before because it just "happens". However, there are several tax implications of becoming a partner. In this chapter I will assume that you are joining a UK partnership and that you are a UK tax resident and UK domiciled.

How will you be taxed?

As an employee you are taxed at source under Pay As You Earn (PAYE) and effectively all your tax and National Insurance Contributions (NIC) are deducted from your monthly salary. The same applies for any bonuses during the year, so your tax and National Insurance (NI) liabilities are taken care of.

There are effectively two types of partners – those that are taxed as if they are employees and those that are taxed as self-employed.

Which category do you fall into?

A partner in a UK LLP

A few years ago, the UK's tax authorities, HM Revenue & Customs (HMRC), brought in legislation known as the salaried member rules. These rules are complex and outside the scope of this chapter but I will provide a brief overview.

A UK LLP registers all its members (partners) with Companies House. The provisions are there to provide certainty and to apply to those members of LLPs that are more like employees than partners.

Salaried member rules

When you first become a member of a UK LLP, the rules will need to be considered and the firm will need to document the results.

As a member of a UK LLP, you will be taxed under PAYE as a salaried member unless you fail one of the following tests:

- Condition A: at least 80 percent of your income is of "disguised salary".
- Condition B: you do not have "significant influence" over the affairs of the LLP.
- Condition C: you have put "capital" into the LLP which is not at least 25 percent of your disguised salary.

If the answer to at least one of the above tests is "no", then you will be taxed as a self-employed partner. Pass all three tests and you will be treated as a salaried member of the LLP and will be taxed under PAYE, along with pension auto-enrolment and benefits in kind. The LLP will have to deal with a number of administration issues and suffer the burden of Employers NIC due on your total reward from the LLP as a salaried member.

Disguised salary

What does the legislation mean by disguised salary? In the main if:

- It is fixed.
- It is variable, but not to the overall profitability of the whole of the LLP.
- It is not affected by the overall profits of the LLP.

If a partner can work out what their profit share is going to be, it's usually disguised salary.

Significant influence

A member will need to have significant influence over the business. Furthermore, it will not be sufficient for the LLP agreement to simply say that the individual has significant influence; it will need to hold true in practice.

Capital

This is all about risk and investing funds into the LLP and will be in line with the LLP agreement. New partners have up to two months from the date they first become a partner of the LLP to contribute their capital; otherwise, the test is revisited, and it is likely that you will pass the test and be treated as a salaried member from the date you became a partner, until a retest is applicable. The key here is therefore to contribute your capital on a timely basis. There is no extension, there are no excuses.

All other retests in relation to this test are based on the capital that has been contributed.

Thinking about the conditions

Conditions A and C are forward-looking, based on reasonable expectation.

Condition A should be tested at the start of the LLP's profit-sharing period, which HMRC expects to be the financial year for most firms. The test looks at the reward each partner expects to earn for the profit-sharing period, and the extent to which it is disguised salary.

Condition C should be tested on 6 April, looking at the reward each partner expects to earn for the year to the following 5 April, and compared with the level of capital subscribed to the firm.

Firms should take care to document their salaried member compliance and retest reviews, to ensure that they are available when HMRC checks a firm's compliance with the legislation. The firm should be quite clear whether you fall into the salaried member rules or not, what you or they need to do to ensure that you fail at least one test, and how you are taxed.

There are other times when the salaried member rules need to be reconsidered and retests undertaken. These include the following:

- When the firm's profit share arrangements change;
- Changes in partnership capital;
- The management structure changes; and
- When a partner's status changes.

Non-UK LLPs and other types of partnerships

For all other partnerships, including general partnerships, if you are an individual and are a salaried partner, you are treated akin to an employee. Otherwise, as an individual, you are a "self-employed" partner.

Salaried members

If you are a salaried partner or member, then life will be similar to that as an employee as far as tax is concerned. If, however, you are a self-employed partner, then read on.

Tax rates

Taxable income is assessed at the following rates, for the current tax year 2023/24, ending 5 April 2024:

	Income band	Tax rate
Basic rate tax	£0 to £37,700	20%
Higher rate tax	£37,701 to £125,140	40%
Additional rate tax	Above £125,140	45%

There is a personal allowance of £12,570 for the current tax year, although this reduces by £1 for every £2 of a partner's income over £100,000. The marginal rate of tax on income between £100,000 and £125,140, when the allowance becomes nil, is therefore 60 percent.

National Insurance Contributions (NIC)

Employees pay NIC via PAYE and the NIC is known as Class 1. Partners will need to pay Class 2 and Class 4 NIC.

Class 2 National Insurance is currently fixed at £3.45 per week, and totals £179.40 for 2023/24. This is calculated on your annual self-assessment tax return and collected as part of your annual income tax liability.

Class 4 National Insurance is profit-related and is calculated as follows for 2023/34:

Amount	Rate
First £12,570	0%
£12,571 to £50,270	9%
Above £50,570	2%

It is calculated on your annual self-assessment tax return and collected as part of your annual income tax liability.

A partner joining or being promoted to partner part-way through the tax year will have paid Class 1 NIC in the tax year. There is a cap on the maximum Class 1, 2, and 4 NIC that is payable in a tax year, and your NIC contributions for the tax year will be adjusted on your tax return if you exceed the maximum.

How you will be assessed for income tax

As previously mentioned, a partner is treated as self-employed for tax purposes and therefore is not subject to the PAYE tax regime that applies to employees and salary partners.

A partner is also not subject to the benefit-in-kind tax legislation, unlike employees and salaried partners who are caught.

A partner is assessed for tax on their share of the firm's taxable profits. What profits and for what period?

Basis period

Back in 2021, the government announced a reform that will change how partnership profits will be assessed from the tax year 2024/25, i.e. from 6 April 2024. This reform, known as the "Basis Period Reform", impacts firms that have an accounting year-end that is not coterminous with the UK fiscal year-end of 5 April.

The impact of this new legislation is that, from 6 April 2024, a partner will be assessed on their profit share for the tax year ending 5 April 2025.

To deal with the reform, the tax year ending 5 April 2024 (2023/24) is treated as a transitional year.

HMRC accepts 31 March (1, 2, 3 and 4 April) as being coterminous with 5 April.

To understand what this means, it is easier to look at a few examples.

Example 1

The firm has an accounting year end of 31 March.

You become a partner on 1 April 2023.

Your taxable profit share for the year ended 31 March 2024, 2025, and 2026 is £200,000, £250,000, and £300,000 respectively.

- For the tax year 2023/24, ending 5 April 2024, you will be taxed on your taxable profit share of £200,000.
- For the tax year 2024/25, ending 5 April 2025, you will be taxed on your taxable profit share of £250,000.
- For the tax year 2025/26, ending 5 April 2026, you will be taxed on your taxable profit share of £300,000.

The accounting year is coterminous to the fiscal year.

Example 2

The firm has an accounting year end of 30 April.

You become a partner on 1 May 2023.

Your taxable profit share for the year ended 30 April 2024, 2025, and 2026 is £200,000, £250,000, and £300,000 respectively.

For the tax year 2023/24, ending 5 April 2024, you will be taxed on:

- Your salary for the month of April 2023; plus
- 11/12 of your taxable profit share for the year ending 30 April 2024, i.e., £183,333 (£200,000 × 11/12).

For the tax year 2024/25, ending 5 April 2025, you will be taxed on:

- 1/12 of your taxable profit share for the year ending 30 April 2024, i.e. £16,667 (£200,000 × 1/12); plus
- 11/12 of your taxable profit share for the year ending 30 April 2025, i.e. £229,167 (£250,000 × 11/12).

For the tax year 2025/26, ending 5 April 2026, you will be taxed on:

- 1/12 of your taxable profit share for the year ending 30 April 2025, i.e. £20,833 (£250,000 × 1/12); plus
- 11/12 of your taxable profit share for the year ending 30 April 2026, i.e. £275,000 (£300,000 × 11/12).

You are taxed on your taxable profits attributable to the UK fiscal year ending 5 April.

Example 3

The firm has an accounting year end of 31 December.

You become a partner on 1 January 2024.

Your taxable profit share for the year ended 31 December 2024, 2025, and 2026 is £200,000, £250,000, and £300,000 respectively.

For the tax year 2023/24, ending 5 April 2024, you will be taxed on:

- Your salary for the nine months from April through to December 2023; plus
- 3/12 of your taxable profit share for the year ending 31 December 2024, i.e., £50,000 (£200,000 × 3/12).

For the tax year 2024/25, ending 5 April 2025, you will be taxed on:

- 9/12 of your taxable profit share for the year ending 31 December 2024, i.e., £150,000 (£200,000 × 9/12); plus
- 3/12 of your taxable profit share for the year ending 31 December 2025, i.e., £62,500 (£250,000 × 3/12).

For the tax year 2025/26, ending 5 April 2026, you will be taxed on:

- 9/12 of your taxable profit share for the year ending 31 December 2025, i.e., £187,500 (£250,000 × 9/12); plus
- 3/12 of your taxable profit share for the year ending 31 December 2026, i.e., £75,000 (£300,000 × 3/12).

You are taxed on your taxable profits attributable to the UK fiscal year ending 5 April.

A partner is taxed on their taxable profits for the basis period, and this is not the accounting profit in that period, nor the profits distributed to them.

If we consider the tax year 2023/24, ending 5 April 2024, and if the firm had an accounting year to 31 March 2024, partners are assessed on their share of the tax adjusted profits for the year ended 31 March 2024. The firm may not have distributed all the profits out to the partners before the accounting year-end. In fact, there may be quite a delay before the profit share is paid out. However, it is the profit share and not the distributions that you have received that are taxable on you. (Employees and salaried partners are taxed on what they receive in a tax year.)

A question to ask is when are profits distributed to partners?

What are the taxable profits?

A partner will receive a share of the firm's accounting profits for the accounting year. The accounting profits are not the same as the firm's taxable profits. There are a number of adjustments that are made to the accounting profits to arrive at the taxable profits. These adjustments fall into two categories:

1. Disallowable expenses – amounts that are not tax deductible.

   For example:

   - Expenses not wholly and exclusively incurred for the business.
   - Disallowed by statute – i.e., entertaining expenditure.
   - Capital in nature and not revenue-related.
   - The partner's personal expenses.

2. Items that are taxed separately – timing differences.

   For example:

   - Depreciation v. capital allowances.
   - Employee bonuses not paid within nine months of the accounting year-end.
   - Employer pension contributions paid after the accounting year-end.

The firm's tax-adjusted profits are allocated in accordance with the firm's accounting profit-share arrangements.

Tax administration

On becoming a new partner, HMRC will need to be notified of the change to self-employed status by completing form SA401.

As a new partner, you will need to file an individual UK self-assessment tax return electronically by 31 January following the end of the tax year. If you would rather file using a paper form, then the filing deadline is 31 October following the end of the tax year.

Therefore, the tax return for the tax year 2023/24, ending 5 April 2024, will need to be filed electronically by 31 January 2025 (and if by paper, by 31 October 2024).

If a tax return is filed late, penalties will be levied by HMRC.

Delay	Penalty
Miss deadline	£100
3-6 months	Daily penalty of £10 per day up to 90 days
6 months	£300 or 5 % of the tax liability if higher
12 months*	£300 or 5 % of the tax liability if higher

**If the tax return is 12 months late and the taxpayer deliberately withholds information, the penalty can be 100 percent of the tax liability or £300 if greater. It may be possible to negotiate a lower penalty.*

Tax payments

As an employee, tax is deducted each month from your salary via PAYE. As a partner, the tax regime is quite different. There are two interim tax instalments for each fiscal year with a balancing payment.

For the 2023/24 tax year, interim instalments are payable on 31 January 2024 and 31 July 2024, with the balancing payment due on 31 January 2025.

Interim instalments – namely first and second payments on account – are calculated based on 50 percent of the previous year's self-assessment income tax and NIC (excluding Class 2) liability.

If it is anticipated that the tax liability from one year to the next is likely to fall, then there is scope to reduce payments on account for the year in question. However, care needs to be taken to ensure that the anticipated payments on account are based on total taxable income for the tax year. If the payments on account are excessively reduced, interest will be levied by HMRC. Therefore, if a reduction claim is made, it is good practice to include a "buffer", as actual figures may not be known.

As a new partner who was previously an employee, it is unlikely you will need to make interim instalments in your first tax year as a partner. Instead, your total tax liability for the tax year in which you became a partner will be due in full by 31 January following the end of the tax year.

Example 4

You become a partner on 1 April 2023.

The firm has an accounting year-end of 31 March.

Your tax and NIC liability for the years ended 31 March 2024 and 2025 is £100,179.40 and £125,179.40 respectively.

Your tax liabilities are as follows:

The tax year 2023/24:

- A balancing payment of £100,179.40.

The tax year 2024/25:

- First payment on account of £50,000.

  Based on 50 percent of the previous year's tax liability, less the class 2 NIC.

  50 percent of (£100,179.40 - £179.40).
- Second payment on account of £50,000.

  Based on 50 percent of the previous year's tax liability less the class 2 NIC.

  50 percent of (£100,179.40 - £179.40).
- A balancing payment of £25,179.40.

  Based on tax liability for 2024/25 less payments on account.

  £125,179.40 - £50,000 - £50,000.

The tax year 2025/26:

- First payment on account of £62,500.

  Based on 50 percent of the previous year's tax liability less the class 2 NIC.

  50 percent of (£125,179.40 - £179.40).
- Second payment on account of £62,500.

  Based on 50 percent of the previous year's tax liability less the class 2 NIC.

  50 percent of (£125,179.40 - £179.40).
- A balancing payment based on the tax liability for 2025/26 less the first and second payments on account totaling £125,000.

To summarize, the payments becoming due are as detailed below.

Payable date	Tax due
31 January 2025:	
Balancing payment for the tax year 2023/24	£100,179.40
First payment on account for the tax year 2024/25	£50,000.00
Total due 31 January 2025	£150,179.40
31 July 2025:	
Second payment on account for the tax year 2024/25	£50,000.00
31 January 2026:	
Balancing payment for the tax year 2024/25	£25,179.40
First payment on account for the tax year 2025/26	£62,500.00
Total due 31 January 2026	£87,679.40
31 July 2026:	
Second payment on account for the tax year 2024/25	£62,500.00

Late paid tax

Interest

If tax is not paid by the due dates, interest will be charged on the unpaid liability and will run from the original due date until the date the tax is paid. The current interest rate is seven percent.

Penalty for late payment of tax

If any tax for a fiscal year-end is paid after the payment date of 31 January following the end of the tax year, then the following penalties will be levied based on the outstanding tax liability:

- 30 days late, a late payment penalty of five percent.
- Six months late, an additional five percent late payment penalty.
- 12 months late, a further five percent late payment penalty.

Tax reserves

Professional firms in the UK predominantly maintain tax reserves on behalf of their partners. This is the amount that the firm holds on your behalf in respect of your future tax liabilities and the firm will settle your future tax liabilities with HMRC as they fall due. This enables partners to focus on what they do best – their work – and leaves the responsibilities of paying the partner's tax liabilities with the firm's finance team. Partners will not therefore need to juggle personal funds to settle tax liabilities around the due dates.

Every firm will have its own tax reserve policy and as a new partner you will need to find out what the firm's policy is and in practical terms what that means for you.

Ask the finance partner or director, does the firm hold tax reserves for partners? And if so, on what basis? The answer should also be found in the partnership agreement.

On whatever basis the firm holds tax reserves on your behalf, these funds will be withheld from your profit share. The firm may estimate a partner's tax liability for reserving purposes in many ways for example, based on:

- Partnership income only (you will need to settle the tax on any personal income).
- Total income of the partner, (i.e., taking into account both partnership and personal income).
- A straight percentage basis, therefore there could be a potential shortfall.

It is therefore essential to understand the basis on which the tax reserves are held and whether sufficient tax reserves will be withheld to settle your future tax liabilities and what element if any you will need to pay personally.

If the firm does not maintain tax reserves on a partner's behalf, you will need to make arrangements to ensure that sufficient funds are put to one side to settle your tax liabilities as they fall due.

International matters

If you join a firm that has offices in overseas jurisdictions, it is likely that you will receive a profit share in connection with that office and as a result will have filing obligations in those countries and pay taxes. On the assumption that you are UK tax resident and domiciled in the UK, you will be taxed on your worldwide income in the UK. That could seem like paying tax twice on the overseas income; however, there is usually scope to claim double tax relief, which effectively means that the tax paid in the other jurisdictions is offset against your UK tax liability.

Partnership capital

Contributing capital in the firm is usually via a loan and loan interest will be paid.

Partners can obtain tax (and NIC) relief on interest paid on any loan taken to subscribe capital to the firm. There are, however, some requirements in this regard, including:

- Relief is only available for so long as you remain a partner of the LLP;
- The funds are used for trading purposes by the LLP; and
- The partner has not withdrawn any capital from the firm.

Where a partner subscribes for capital out of personal funds (either by payment from their own resources or by transfer from a current account) any loan subsequently taken to match this personally subscribed capital is excluded for the purpose of obtaining tax relief on interest providing capital to the firm.

There are exercises that can be undertaken for the member to withdraw their previously invested capital, to then be required to invest fresh capital in the firm and to take a borrowing to fund such investment. HMRC has challenged such transactions and has been successful in doing so. Therefore, advice should be taken to ensure that the refinancing enables tax relief to be available on future loan interest.

Relationship with your mortgage, other loans, and savings

If you are looking to make loan repayments, consider all of your loans and repay the loan with the highest interest rate, after taking into account tax relief. Also, reflect on how you could gainfully employ those funds in other ways to achieve a superior rate of return.

Benefits

As an employee you may have received a number of benefits, including a company car, private medical insurance, life assurance, permanent health insurance, and pension contributions. As a partner, you may have to sort these out yourself, or at least replace some of the benefits. You will therefore need to consider to what extent they are replaced and whether they meet your requirements. Many firms will offer private medical insurance and life assurance and either provide that as part of your profit share or deduct it from your profit share. You will therefore need to find out what is covered and whether it is adequate. For company cars, you may be able to acquire the car from the firm, or if there is a partner car scheme, transfer the car into that scheme. There will be no more employer contributions into your pension scheme. You will therefore need to think about the timing and level of your future pension contributions.

Pension contributions

For employees, it is usual for firms and individuals to pay into a pension scheme. On becoming a partner, this becomes your own responsibility and you will have to make your own contributions. It is therefore worth mentioning what the annual allowance is for contributing to a pension scheme and the tax reliefs available.

The starting point with regards to your annual allowance for pensions is £60,000 gross (£48,000 net) from 6 April 2023. However, for those earning over £260,000, the annual allowance reduces by £1 for every £2 of income over £260,000 down to a minimum allowance of £10,000 gross (£8,000 net) at an income of £360,000 or more. For tax years prior to 2023/24, the annual allowance, restricted annual allowance, and earnings thresholds were lower.

There is also scope to utilize unused annual allowance capacity from the preceding three tax years, using the earliest year first, on the basis that there was a policy in place during those years. The current year's annual allowance must be utilized first. For the 2023/24 tax year, you would need to use all your annual allowance for the year before being able to utilize any unused allowances from 2020/21, 2021/22, and 2022/23.

Care needs to be taken when making pension contributions as, if excessive contributions are made, no tax relief is available, and a pensions savings tax charge will result.

When you contribute into your pension scheme, you make a payment net of tax, and the pension scheme provider will claim the basic rate tax back from the UK tax authorities. Furthermore, you will receive further tax relief by making a claim on your tax return, which will reduce your tax liability.

Example 5

You contribute £8,000 into your pension.

The pension scheme provider will claim £2,000 (£8,000 × 25 percent) back from the tax authorities.

The total amount paid into your pension scheme is therefore £10,000.

The amount of tax relief you then claim via your tax return will be as follows:

	Tax relief claimed	
Basic rate taxpayer	£0	£10,000 x (20% - 20%)
Higher rate taxpayer	£2,000	£10,000 x (40% - 20%)
Additional rate taxpayer	£2,500	£10,000 x (45% - 20%)

Summary

As a piece of advice, make sure you know who you need to touch base with in respect of partner taxation affairs. Ask any questions that you have, but also ensure that you provide the information they require to manage your taxation affairs in a timely manner. Their information will flow into the cash management of the firm and cashflow forecasts. They are the ones that in the majority of cases will arrange for your tax to be paid to the relevant authorities.

Finally, when you are required to pay partnership capital, don't dally as you may inadvertently end up becoming a salaried member, which will give rise to additional costs for the firm and higher taxes for you as an individual.

Chapter 12:
Wellbeing and partnership in law firms – challenges and opportunities

By Jean-Baptiste Lebelle, head of HR, Allen & Overy

Introduction

Wellbeing is a concept that refers to the state of being healthy, happy, and fulfilled in the physical, mental, emotional, social, and spiritual aspects of life. Wellbeing is not only influenced by individual factors, such as personality, values, and goals, but also environmental factors, such as family, friends, community, and of course work.

In law firms, this concept has evolved significantly in recent years, as the legal profession faces increasing challenges of stress, burnout, mental health issues, and ethical dilemmas. Traditionally, wellbeing in law firms was largely equated with financial success, productivity, and reputation, often at the expense of personal health, happiness, and values. However, a growing body of research, advocacy, and best practices supported by strong HR professionals has highlighted the importance of fostering a culture of wellbeing in law firms, especially since the COVID-19 pandemic. This major event posed unprecedented challenges and disruptions to all professions, affecting the mental and physical health, productivity, and morale of employees. Every law firm, therefore, should put wellbeing at the heart of its people strategy, especially for partners. Wellbeing is not a one-size-fits-all concept, but a subjective and multidimensional experience that varies from person to person, and from situation to situation.

Wellbeing – a continuing challenge for partners in a complex and moving environment

Pursuing a career as a partner in a business law firm is not for everyone – besides the prerequisites in terms of technical, relational, commercial, and managerial skills, partners have to show an exceptionally high level of dedication and loyalty to their work, which they normally agree to do because of the generous financial benefits they receive.

It is generally estimated that one associate in ten who joins a law firm will make a career as a partner. Those who choose another professional destiny are often motivated by the fear of sacrificing their quality of life (stress, workload, family life). It is therefore fundamental when choosing to become a partner to have thought about the challenge of wellbeing and to give oneself the means to overcome it.

There is no doubt that the legal profession is one of the most stressful and competitive sectors, especially for partners. Partners have to deal with complex and demanding issues, tight deadlines, high standards, and ethical dilemmas. They have to manage their teams (taking into consideration the expectations of the new generation), their clients, their financial performance, and their reputation. They have to balance their work and their life, and cope with the uncertainty and ambiguity of the legal market.

Furthermore, the legal sector is a complex and moving environment that has undergone significant changes in recent years, driven by various factors such as globalization, digitalization, regulation, and client demand. Lawyers have embraced new technologies and tools to enhance their efficiency, communication, and innovation, including artificial intelligence, cloud computing, online platforms, and legal design. Furthermore, lawyers have faced increasing competition and pressure from alternative legal service providers, such as consultants, accountants, and paralegals, who offer lower costs, greater flexibility, and specialized expertise. Additionally, lawyers have responded to the changing needs and expectations of their clients, who seek more value, transparency, and collaboration, as well as social and environmental responsibility. Therefore, the legal sector has evolved enormously in recent years, requiring lawyers to be more versatile, adaptable, and creative than ever before.

Working from home has also become widely adopted among the legal profession. With the aid of technology, such as video conferencing, cloud-based platforms, and digital signatures, lawyers can communicate with clients, colleagues, and courts, access and share documents, and conduct research and drafting from their home offices. However, remote working can have negative effects on lawyer wellbeing. Challenges such as isolation, blurred boundaries, communication difficulties, and ergonomic risks are often underestimated. Therefore, it is important to understand and anticipate the impact of this new organisational dynamic on mental health.

Wellbeing is not a static state, but a dynamic and ongoing process that requires attention and adaptation. During their careers, partners need to constantly monitor and adjust their wellbeing levels, as they face different challenges and opportunities in their professional and personal lives. We often hear that a career as a partner in a law firm is more like a marathon than a sprint, as you need to be extremely resilient in the long-term to achieve sustainable performance. It is not only about physical health, but also mental, emotional, and social aspects.

Partners have multiple roles and responsibilities, but also rewards and opportunities. Being a partner is not only a job, but also a career, a vocation, and almost a lifestyle. They have to be passionate about their work. Usually, partners enjoy a high level of autonomy, recognition, influence, and income. They have the chance to work on challenging and meaningful cases, to develop their expertise and reputation, and to make a positive impact on society. They have the opportunity to grow and learn, to collaborate and network, and to mentor and inspire others. In that regard, this is definitely a position able to provide success and fulfilment.

On the other hand, high expectations, competition, long hours, and pressure can harm partners' wellbeing, affect mental health, and even lead to burnout. Burnout and fatigue due to heavy workloads are both forms of stress-related exhaustion, but they have different causes and consequences. Fatigue is a temporary state of physical and mental tiredness that results from exceeding one's capacity to cope with the demands and pressures of work. It can be alleviated by reducing the workload, taking breaks, having sufficient resources, resting, and engaging in self-care activities. Burnout, on the other hand, is a chronic and severe condition of emotional, mental, and physical depletion that results from prolonged exposure to work-related stressors that are perceived as overwhelming, uncontrollable, or meaningless. It is characterized by a loss of motivation, enthusiasm, and satisfaction with work, as well as by symptoms of depression, anxiety, cynicism, detachment, and reduced performance. It can have serious negative impacts on one's health, wellbeing, and relationships, and it requires professional help and a significant change in one's work environment and lifestyle.

Partners often face unrealistic and conflicting demands – from themselves, from their clients, from their peers, and from their family. They may feel overwhelmed, exhausted, frustrated, or isolated. They may experience physical symptoms, such as headaches, insomnia, or intense fatigue. They may suffer from mental and emotional issues, such as anxiety, depression, or low self-esteem. They may lose their motivation, their creativity, their passion, or their sense of purpose. This huge level of stress leads some people to use alcohol and illicit substances to try to overcome their fatigue and regain their performance level. That can explain the drinking culture in some law firms. According to a 2016 study by the American Bar Association (ABA), lawyers have higher rates of alcohol and substance misuse than other professionals.[1]

Wellbeing should be seen as a holistic and comprehensive concept that encompasses the partners' cognitive, affective, and relational dimensions. It is about how partners think, feel, and interact with themselves and others. It is also about partners' satisfaction, happiness, and fulfilment in their work and their life. The key challenge for a partner is the ability to cope with stress, to express their emotions and share their difficulties, and to build their resilience.

Resources and strategies for partner wellbeing

Wellbeing is a shared responsibility between partners and the firm and depends on individual and organizational factors. Partners and the firm have a mutual interest and a mutual obligation to promote and protect partners' wellbeing. Partners have to take charge of their own wellbeing, by identifying their needs, values, and goals, and by adopting healthy and sustainable behaviours and attitudes. The firm has to provide a conducive and supportive work environment, by offering resources, policies, culture, and leadership that foster partner wellbeing. Partners and the firm have to communicate and cooperate, to address the challenges and opportunities of wellbeing, and to create a positive and productive work culture.

The impact of wellbeing and mental health on productivity should not be underestimated, especially for partners – a position that demands high levels of performance and resilience.

Several factors contribute to the wellbeing of partners, including autonomy, competence, relatedness, recognition, feedback, mentoring, learning, and diversity. These factors enable partners to feel self-determined, capable, connected, valued, supported, challenged, and respected in their work environment, which fosters their intrinsic motivation and psychological needs.

Partners should also be role models for associates in every dimension, including wellbeing and work–life balance. In a law firm, partners have the most important influence on the culture, values, and expectations of the organization, as well as on the development, performance, and satisfaction of the associates who work with them. Therefore, it is essential that partners also act as role models for associates in every dimension, including wellbeing and work–life balance. By doing so, they can foster a positive and supportive environment that promotes the health, happiness, and productivity of everyone involved.

To be role models for associates in terms of wellbeing and work–life balance, to foster a new culture, partners should demonstrate and encourage particular behaviours and practices including:

- Speaking up and sharing mental health struggles and challenges with peers and teams in order to build a healthy and supportive work environment. Do not fear showing weakness and asking for advice.
- Balancing the demands and priorities of work and personal life and respecting the work–life preferences and boundaries of associates and clients. For example, demonstrate that everyone deserves to leave the office early without guilt when possible.
- Disconnecting during holidays and making the most of their holidays and sabbatical leave.
- Taking care of their own physical, mental, and emotional health, and seeking help when needed.
- Engaging in activities and hobbies that enrich their lives and bring them joy and fulfilment.
- Setting realistic and clear goals and expectations and providing regular and constructive feedback and recognition.
- Communicating openly and honestly and listening actively and empathetically to the concerns and opinions of associates and clients.
- Delegating effectively and empowering associates to take ownership and initiative in their work, providing them with the necessary resources and support.

By being role models for associates in wellbeing and work–life balance, partners can not only enhance their own and others' wellbeing, but also create a competitive advantage for the firm in attracting, retaining, and developing talent, and in delivering excellence and value to clients.

However, a wellbeing policy tailored for partners faces significant challenges and barriers, stemming from the intense, demanding, and high-stakes nature of the legal profession, the firm's competitive and hard-driving culture, the scarcity of time, resources, and support, the stigma and fear of exposing vulnerability or weakness, the inertia and opposition to change, and the challenge of measuring and evaluating the effectiveness of wellbeing initiatives. These challenges can hinder the adoption and effectiveness of a wellbeing policy and can create scepticism, resentment, or indifference among the partners.

Therefore, it is important to find possible solutions and best practices to overcome these challenges, such as:

- Involve the partners in the design, implementation, and evaluation of the wellbeing policy, to ensure their input, feedback, and buy-in.
- Communicate the rationale, goals, and benefits of the wellbeing policy, to raise awareness, understanding, and commitment.
- Provide a variety of wellbeing programs, activities, and resources, to cater to the different needs, preferences, and interests of the partners.
- Create a supportive and trusting culture, where wellbeing is valued, encouraged, and rewarded, and where partners can share their experiences, challenges, and successes without fear of judgment or retaliation.
- Monitor and assess the outcomes and impacts of the wellbeing policy, to identify the strengths, weaknesses, and areas for improvement, and to celebrate and recognize the achievements and contributions of the partners.

Wellbeing requires a holistic and multidimensional approach with concrete initiatives

Achieving and sustaining wellbeing as a partner in a professional services firm requires a holistic and multidimensional approach that encompasses both personal and organizational dimensions, and that is supported by concrete and consistent initiatives. In this section, we will discuss some of the key initiatives that can enhance the wellbeing of partners and that can be implemented at different levels, such as individual, team, firm, and network. These initiatives are not exhaustive or prescriptive, but rather illustrative and suggestive, and can be adapted and customized according to the specific needs, contexts, and cultures of each partner and firm.

Promoting the concept of optimal busyness

As the workload of partners is always a challenge in law firms (fast-paced settings where long hours, intense work, and billable hours are the norm), it is extremely important to address this issue by promoting the concept of "optimal busyness" rather than "excessive busyness". Optimal busyness refers to the optimal level of workload, activity, and stimulation that allows partners to perform at their best, while maintaining their wellbeing and happiness. Optimal busyness is a productive and enjoyable state of work that varies depending on the situation and the individual. It involves a balance of different factors that affect the work experience, such as challenge, skill, autonomy, support, variety, and routine.

Excessive busyness refers to the excessive level of workload, activity, and stimulation that impairs partners' performance, wellbeing, and happiness. It is obvious that, depending on emergencies, client demands, or unforeseen events, a partner will inevitably be – at some point or another – in a state of excessive busyness. It is unrealistic to deny it, but it is important to find a balance and to position oneself again in the optimal zone. In the same way, there will be moments when the partner will operate in his or her comfort zone and this can present some drawbacks.

Being aware and attentive to these different phases allows a partner to regain control over his or her activity and performance in the long-term. See Figure 1.

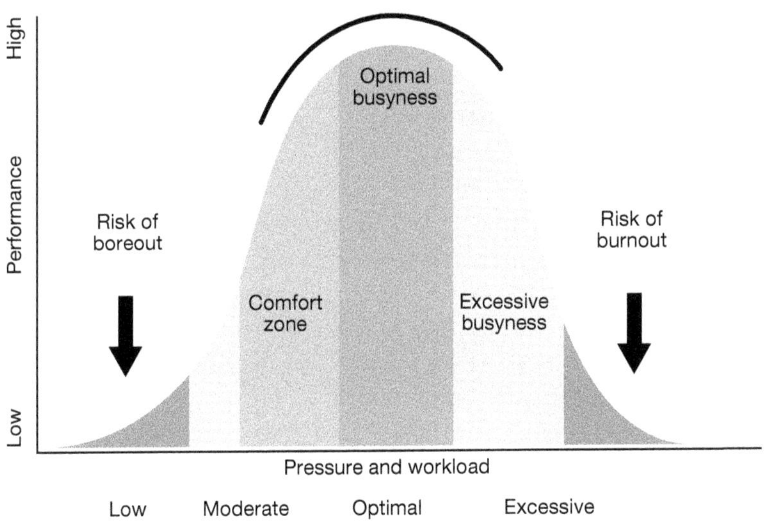

Figure 1: Optimal vs excessive busyness.

Promoting the concept of optimal busyness can help partners avoid the trap of equating busyness with success, status, or value, and instead focus on the quality, impact, and meaning of their work. It can also help partners challenge and change the norms, expectations, and behaviours that drive and reward excessive busyness within the firm, and create a more sustainable and healthy work culture.

Partners – but also the firm as an organisation – need to manage their workload and work environment to maintain optimal busyness and prevent boredom, stress, or burnout. The boundary between excessive busyness and its harmful consequences is very thin and depends on many factors.

This is why coaching and mentoring are crucial to help partners balance their work and avoid burnout.

Provide mentoring, coaching, and feedback

An essential initiative for wellbeing is seeking and providing mentorship, coaching, feedback, and recognition among partners. Mentorship and coaching can help people navigate the complex and demanding roles and responsibilities of being a partner, and provide them with guidance, support, and advice on various aspects of their career and life. Feedback and recognition can help partners assess their performance, identify their strengths and areas for improvement, and acknowledge their contributions and achievements. These initiatives can also foster a culture of learning, collaboration, and appreciation within the firm, and enhance the sense of belonging and trust among partners.

Define and align the partner's personal vision and values with those of their firm

Another project that could enhance wellbeing is developing a personal vision and values for one's career and life and aligning them with the firm's mission and culture. Having a personal vision and values can help partners define their purpose, direction, and meaning, and guide their decisions and actions. Aligning them with the firm's mission and culture can help partners ensure that they are working for a cause and an organization that they believe in, and that they are contributing to a positive and impactful social and environmental change. In that regard, pro bono initiatives, which consist of providing free professional services to non-profit organizations or disadvantaged individuals, can help to restore meaning to one's daily commitment, by creating connections with change-makers and contributing to projects with high social or environmental impact. These initiatives allow meaning to be restored to the lawyer's profession, especially for those who earn a lot. These initiatives can also help partners enhance their motivation, engagement, and satisfaction, and foster a sense of coherence and congruence between their personal and professional identities.

Creating and fostering a supportive and inclusive work environment

A supportive and inclusive work environment can help partners feel safe, respected, and valued, and enable them to bring their whole selves to work. It can also help partners embrace and leverage the diversity of perspectives, backgrounds, and identities within the firm, and enhance the creativity, innovation, and performance of the firm. Creating and fostering a supportive and inclusive work environment can be achieved by implementing policies, practices, and initiatives that promote diversity, equity, and belonging, and by cultivating a culture of empathy, compassion, and respect among partners.

Encouraging and participating in social and professional networks

Much like sharing insight and resources and finding role models, allies, and sponsors can be very impactful on wellbeing, networking should be encouraged as a firm policy. Participating in social and professional networks, communities of practice, and affinity groups can help partners build and maintain meaningful and supportive relationships, both within and outside the firm, and enhance their social and emotional wellbeing. They can also help partners access and exchange valuable information, knowledge, and opportunities, and enhance their professional and personal development. These networks, communities, and groups can be facilitated by the firm, or initiated by the partners themselves, and can be based on various criteria, such as interests, goals, roles, or identities.

Recognizing and rewarding achievements

Both individually and collectively, recognizing and rewarding achievement and acknowledging and learning from failures and challenges is important. Celebrating and rewarding achievements, milestones, and successes can help partners recognize and appreciate their efforts and results and boost their morale and confidence. It can also help partners share and celebrate their accomplishments and contributions with their clients, colleagues, and stakeholders, and enhance their reputation and relationships. Acknowledging and learning from failures and challenges can help partners cope with and overcome the difficulties and setbacks that they encounter and turn them into opportunities for improvement and growth. It can also help partners develop a growth mindset, a resilient attitude, and a learning culture within the firm.

Conclusion

Implementing a true wellbeing strategy for partners and transforming law firm culture to better support mental health can not only improve partner wellbeing, but also create a positive ripple effect whereby partners are seen as role models for their peers, associates, clients, and the whole legal profession. Wellbeing and partnership status are not only compatible, but also complementary and beneficial for all stakeholders. Furthermore, wellbeing is now widely seen as essential for the success and sustainability of law firms, as it affects the quality and quantity of the work, the health and happiness of the lawyers, and the reputation and profitability of the firm.

It is time to take care of partners' wellbeing in a genuine manner. This will require time, sustained effort, and focus, but the next generation of legal professionals will strongly advocate for this issue and may transform the industry profoundly.

References

1 www.americanbar.org/news/abanews/publications/youraba/2017/december-2017/secrecy-and-fear-of-stigma-among-the-barriers-to-lawyer-well-bei/

About Globe Law and Business

Globe Law and Business was established in 2005. From the very beginning, we set out to create legal books that are sufficiently high level to be of real use to the experienced professional, yet still accessible and easy to navigate. Most of our authors are drawn from Magic Circle and other top commercial firms, both in the United Kingdom and internationally.

Our titles are carefully produced, with the utmost attention paid to editorial, design and production processes. We hope this results in high-quality publications that are easy to read and a pleasure to own.

In 2021, we were very pleased to announce the start of a new chapter for Globe Law and Business following the acquisition of law books under the imprint Ark Publishing. Our law firm management list is now significantly expanded with many well known and loved Ark Publishing titles.

We are also pleased to announce the launch of our online content platform, Globe Law Online. This allows for easy search and networked access across firms. Key collections include the Legal Content Collection (including a Private Client module) and the Law Firm Management Collection. Details of all titles included can be found at www.globelawonline.com. Email glo@globelawandbusiness.com for further details and to arrange a free trial for you or your firm.

We'd very much like to hear from you with your thoughts and ideas for improving what we offer. Please do feel free to email me on sian@globelawandbusiness.com. Happy reading and thank you for your time.

Sian O'Neill
Managing director
Globe Law and Business
www.globelawandbusiness.com

www.ingramcontent.com/pod-product-compliance
Ingram Content Group UK Ltd.
Pitfield, Milton Keynes, MK11 3LW, UK
UKHW021849150926
8657IPUK00005B/160